The Coyote Laffed

103 Short Stories

By
B & B Christenson

Copyright # 470546
Copyright © 1998 by B & B Christenson

The Coyote Laffed

I.S.B.N 1-55056-652-0

Canadian Cataloguing in Publication Data

Christenson, B. (Bernie), 1925-

The coyote laffed [sic]

Includes index.

1. Frontier and pioneer life--Canada, Western--Anecdotes. 2. Frontier and pioneer life--West (U.S.)--Anecdotes. 3. Pioneers--Canada, Western--Anecdotes. 4. Pioneers--West (U.S.)--Anecdotes. I. Christenson, B. (Berniece), 1927- II. Title. III. Title: The coyote laughed.

FC3237.C48 1999   971.2'02   C98-920225-9
F1060.38.C48 1999

Cover layout
        Glen T. Christenson
Editors
        Leroy & Rhonda Christenson
Author
        Bernie Christenson
Illustrator
        Berniece Christenson
Printed and Bound in Canada by
        Friesens Printers
        Altona, Manitoba

Acknowledgments

The late Flora Puckett, Woodrow Newton and Eldy Sproxton were the first to lend encouragement.
Later, Allison Muri, Jerry Doll Jr., and other relatives and family added inducement.
For proof reading and rereading, we are indebted to Anita Froyman.

Bernie C.

Guidance from my early teachers, Joyce Theaker and Myra Shepperdson, has helped to make my art contribution possible.

Berniece C.

To a person that revels in finding literary or grammatical errors, this book may be a gold mine.
To others, if you find a smile, a laugh or a memory, you've found its meaning.

B.C.

Table of Contents

The Salesman 1

The Chief's Wife 4

Tarp the Hound 5

Old Horse Buyer & Seller 8

Easy Credit 9

How-To Books 12

Knot-Head Mare 15

Bad Money 18

Luck, Plus Or Minus 24

Travelling in Montana 26

An Actor? 29

The Parade 32

Grandma Maria 34

The Last Bite 36

The Good Life 39

The Watch Dog 42

The Ranch Lady 44

Ownership 46

Don't do it Lady 49

The Zane Grey Man 50

Beaver 53

Bad Brakes 56

Compromise 59

Chuck 61

Looking Back 64

They Tried Harder 67

To Gain Experience 69

A Cup Full 73

That Must Have Hurt 75

One Tree 77

Mapping the Backwoods 79

For a Cup of Tea 81

From the Daily Paper 84

Ski Slope 86

The Red Car 89

We Tried 91

Blueprint 93

Keeping Up 95

The Babysitter 97

Goldie 100

Hagen's Horses 102

Bear Scare 104

Home 106

Saskatoon Berries 107

Buying Bob 110

Old Bones 113

Black Powder 116

Braddock 120

Big Brothers 122

Passing Through 126

It's Not All Roses 129

No Change 131

Big Worry 133

The Sheep Men 135

Poor Pete 138

The End of the Devil 141

Driving Lessons 143

Home Improvements 146

Meat in the Pot 148

The Road North 150

Dance Class 153

Language Lesson 155

Water Holes 157

Hotel 158

Science With Luck 160

The Lost Art 163

Fearsome Trip 165

The Feeling 167

A Friend 169

One More Gone 171

Hard as Flint 174

Lonesome 176

Homesteading 178

Tall Grass 181

Memory Lane 182

Our Mistake 184

Moving 186

Pie Face 188

A Wee Bit O' Privacy 190

Profit 192

Santa 196

Movie Script 198

The Sleigh 202

A Prairie Town 205

Mach 1 208

Spike 210

Shorty L 215

Poor Horse 218

Abe 220

Storm 224

Just Talk 226

Taxi 227

Teeth 230

Speeding Ticket 232

Safety Measures 234

Good, Bad and Others 237

What Were They? 242

Absolute Zero 245

Slippery Sam 247

Farmers 249

The Black Mare 251

The Road Block 253

The Coyote Laffed 255

The Salesman

It was on a Saturday afternoon in September, that I wandered into the garage behind Tom and Em's house in Lethbridge, Alberta. Tom was giving a '57 Dodge a complete tune up. Points, plugs, carb, -- well, the whole works. I leaned on one fender or the other of the Dodge, as he told of his youthful days in southern Saskatchewan.

His father, David Mayne, was a member of the North West Mounted Police. In the Regina office he was handed a wanted poster of a person accused of murder. "Bring in this man," was the only order given, and this was in the dead of winter. If there is a record of the chase and arrest, it would be buried in the archives in Ottawa, Ontario.

About two years after the command "Bring him in" was given, Officer Mayne brought his prisoner to be locked up in the police cells at Dawson City in the Yukon Territory. When the prisoner was secured, David's needs were to be looked after. The regulation one ounce of whiskey was given.

"That warmed my throat, how about another?", he asked.

"No! You received the regular allotment. And look at your dress - britches torn, tunic threadbare, tears in your coat and holes in your boots. Your appearance is a disgrace to the force!" The detachment commander heaped on more ridicule.

After tracking a man across the prairie, over the mountains, through the forest and all the way to the Yukon in a steady two year hunt, this reprimand did not sit well. The skin on his face was peeling, his hands and feet were so pained by the cold that they were nearly useless to him. As Officer Mayne stood at attention for the dressing down, he had but one thought, "To - - - - with the police force."

It was early spring when Officer Mayne, with his prisoner, reported in at the Regina barracks. He received more respect there than he did in the Yukon. With his discharge and accumulated pay, that he'd had no time to spend while on the man hunt, he was ready for the next turn of his life. He bought a horse and saddle.

1

On checking with the authorities of the Assiniboia Territory about establishing a ranch, he was told, "Go and find a spot and settle down." A few days of riding brought him near Seventeen-mile Butte. There, in 1903, he built his ranch, married and started to raise a family.

One late fall day in 1912, rancher Mayne had gone to Montana. There, the railroad construction camp was being shut down for the winter. All of the horses were sold or kept, but the mules were not. What a sorry herd of animals! Blistered shoulders, harness rubbed sores, cuts, scratches, bruises, even wounds. This poor group of animals was to be destroyed. The railroad people had gotten their value out of them. Rancher Mayne purchased the whole herd for a song. He hired a few cowboys to get them up the trail into Canada and to the home ranch.

The first job was to get the shoes off of the mules. After that, the winter was spent curing the sores and feeding them hay. Grazing on good pasture for the summer, the mules had a new lease on life and looked the part.

With the Great World War on, the Red Cross could sure use some help. Thus, Rancher Mayne tagged a group of Regina's professional men, "If you gentlemen will buy an ambulance and the harness, I will provide a six-mule hitch." Each man was only too glad to do such a patriotic thing.

In due time the ambulance was in Regina. The harness was procured locally, and it was of the best. The mules arrived from the ranch in a highly polished condition. When this outfit was all assembled and posed for pictures on Eleventh Avenue it caused a stir. "Beautiful, Patriotic, Just great," and so went the praise of the public for these most generous citizens who were being so good to the Red Cross and its war work.

An army officer, stiff with medals, asked, "Where did you find six mules so evenly matched?"

"I have more like them out at the ranch," Mr. Mayne informed the military man.

"Would you sell some of them to the army?"

"Well, it will be some job to round them all up. We couldn't do that to sell just a few," Mayne replied.

"Get them in and we will have a look at your mules."

Days later, the army men arrived at the ranch near Seventeen-mile Butte. Inspecting mules in the large corral, the officer noted that quite a few had white hairs around their eyes.

Rancher Mayne was out to sell mules. "Yes, some show their age, but when you get them to France that won't matter a darn little bit."

"True enough, it's their work ability that we need," the officer conceded and then asked, "How much per animal?"

Mayne gave this some serious thought. If he had paid three bucks for a mule three years ago, all he had to do was add two zeroes to the first figure and there was the price. "That is rather costly, but we'll pick out a few," the old soldier said.

The rancher countered that one, "You couldn't find this many good mules if you travelled all across Canada."

"True, true," was his military view.

"If you want to pick just a few the price will be a lot higher than I said," Mayne went on. "Why don't you people stay with us tonight, and tomorrow we'll help you get the mules to the railway pen in Moose Jaw?"

Some more faint haggling, because an army officer cannot be out done by a back-in-the-hills rancher.

Mr. Mayne said, "We can open the gate and let them out. You can go and buy some cheaper mules elsewhere."

"Now don't be hasty!" The officer knew that Canada was not overrun by mules, and here he had found a gold mine.

David Mayne had the last word, "In the morning we'll get them on the trail to the city. When we get there, you give me an army voucher for one hundred and ninety-six mules." They shook hands on the deal.

The Chief's Wife

We lived near the southwest edge of the Chitek Lake Indian Reserve. We had to cross the reserve to get off the ranch.

With two fields of hay cut and windrowed, it rained every day for two weeks. On Thursday morning I drove to town, the sun was out bright and clear. The beautiful bright weather eased my thoughts of molding cow feed.

On the road home, I came to an old, green half ton truck. Its owner had a dark shawl and a blue sweater and was standing between her truck and the new, red ford car that belonged to Chief Leo Thomas and his wife, Miriam. By the time I had stopped behind the west bound vehicle, the owner had climbed in and motored off down the road. Miriam moved her car forward and stopped abreast of me.

"Isn't this just a gorgeous day?" was her greeting.

After chatting for a few minutes, I mentioned that if the wet weather returned I would have to find a really high bridge and jump off.

With just a bit of a mischievous smile she said, "Would you please take Leo along with you? He is about ready for a trip like that." With a happy wave of her hand, and a smile as bright as the day, she drove away.

Tarp the Hound

There was not a thing that I needed in the mall. That's why I was comfortably soaking in the sunshine on a bench by a palm tree. In time, I shared the bench with a tall, thin gentleman about my age. His clothes were that of a visitor to the sun belt, but just a wee bit different. The straw hat was not local, nor were his shoes. He must have seen the same in me.

"You from the Dakotas?" He asked.

"I'm from Canada," I answered.

We sat in silence for a while. Two Hispanic kids, a boy about four and his sister, somewhat older, came along with a mite sized mutt on a heavy cotton cord. The leash was knotted around the pups neck so it also served as a collar. Sometimes the boy led the dog and then the dog led the boy. The girl ran behind and supervised her brother and their snoopy little pooch.

"Ever have a dog?", my neighbour asked.

"Yes, we had several on the ranch. A couple of them I'll never forget," I said.

"I had one, some years back. He was a good one."

This time he looked right at me. His blue-gray eyes were nearly hidden in a squint. His long face had been shaved with a razor with a notch in the blade. In some places the little white whiskers seemed to be in narrow rows.

"Ya, I had a good ol' boy we called Tarp. He got that name because he could cover any situation. When Ma wanted a frying chicken, she would tell Tarp and he would bring a young rooster to the wood pile where Ma stood with the axe. If she wanted a roaster, he would get a fat old hen. Oh, he was good. One time I turned down a hundred and fifty cart wheels for him.

One day I come in from a coon hunt, and my pocketbook was missing. I said 'Tarp go get it.' The sun was just over the mountain when here come Tarp with my billfold.

5

A mining company found coal on my farm, they wanted to buy me out but I made them a deal to lease the coal seam on the side of the mountain. I get a percentage and they get around a bunch of government rules. It's a good deal for both of us, and I still farm the bottomland. When the mine guys came, they had a dog. Well right off ol' Tarp goes and marks off his ground. You know he'd pee a squirt at a bush and a rock and a tree and so on till he had a circle done up. That was to let all dogs know that it was Tarp's place and no trespassing.

One day the mine dog chased a rabbit close to Tarp's line. Golly be hanged if my dog didn't go and mark off the whole side of the mountain as his.

I had to go over to the county seat one time. Tarp was with me, riding in the box of the pickup. Now that is a pretty big place, the county seat. I parked along the Court House square and left the dog in the truck.

I didn't know that my neighbour Herm was there. He was sittin' on a park bench while his son Bob was at the bank to borrow some green to tide him over till he sold some fresh sawed pine boards. He told me how smart Tarp was.

The dog sat and watched the people stand at the stop light, then go across the square or up the street. Now Tarp wanted some of that park for himself, but couldn't get that far from the truck. So he went to the stop light and started putting his mark on the legs of people going across the square. The men didn't even notice. One cute girl blushed like crazy and let it go at that. A big, old sour lady stood waiting for the light to change when Tarp marked her. Herm said she kicked poor old Tarp so hard in the rear end that he saw some fur fly off the dog. Then Tarp got back in the truck and licked his wounds.

About that time I figured if Tarp was worth a hundred and fifty, his pups could easily be worth a hundred dollars. At eight pups to a litter, and he was a strong dog, so three litters a week, that would come to twenty four hundred. Maybe one litter would be nine, so for easy figuring it would come to twenty five hundred a week. That would be ten thousand a month, more or less.

At the county seat I went to the animal shelter and picked out a female that seemed to be real smart. I kept her in the cab going home. Tarp didn't seem to care. At home he still did not snap out of his slump.

6

For weeks he just moped around. He had no interest in the new dog at all.

One day I come up behind Tarp when he was relieving himself at the gate post. Holy cats, he was as smooth as the female, no lumps at all on his rear end. It was more than fur that Herm saw flying."

I have often thought, how sad! To think one angry lady could kick the foundation right out from under a budding fortune.

Old Horse
Buyer & Seller

Wednesday, June 3, 1903

"That's the one I want."
"Non, Monsieur, he don't look so good."

Thursday, June 4, 1903

"That horse you sold me yesterday is blind."
"Oui, Monsieur, I say he don't look so good."

Easy Credit

When the western prairies were filling with land seekers, they were also filling with machinery dealers. Credit was easy to come by, but repayment wasn't. I think that too many farmers over estimated their income. That would be the reason for the army of bill collectors to cover the prairie. International Harvester Company collectors seemed to have the most undesirable reputation.

On the other hand, the debtors developed many a ruse to avoid face to face meetings. When the little black Ford coup with the square body came down the trail, it was time to run for cover. In one such case, the near penniless farmer ran to his outhouse and hooked the door on the inside. If all was well, his wife would call after the collector had left and the farmer would emerge. On this day she did not call. The good woman explained to the International man that her husband was in the outhouse. Said collector tried to conduct business through a closed door. It boiled down to talking to a closed door. It was either the threat of storm clouds, or hunger, that made the collector go away, and that released the poor prisoner from the little house.

"Get your hand out of my pocket. You're as bad as an International Harvester collector," the uncle scolded his four year old nephew.

What was so repulsive about international collectors? That question stayed with me until Mr. Simonson told my Grandpa the details of his experience.

The Simonson brothers, Roy and Zack, were out in the harvest field. Zack ran his thumb nail around the label that was also the seal on a box of Copenhagen snuff. With the lid in his left hand and the round box in the other, he offered his brother a chew. Roy, with a three-fingered pinch, took half the snuff for his chew. Zack managed the balance and reamed out the corners by running one finger around the inside of the box. It was empty so he tossed it into the fire box of the steam engine. With the tobacco hunger satisfied, Zack went back to look

9

after the threshing machine. This giant was gobbling up wheat sheaves as fast as four men could fork them into the long feeder. Roy sat in the cab of the big steam engine, keeping an eye on its gauges.

The three grain haulers, each with a wagon drawn by four horses, were busy guys. They had to haul the grain to the farm yard and shovel it into the bin. At the start of the season the threshing was being done on the far side of the farm and it was not practical to haul the grain to town. That would be done later on, when they had more time. Into this busy scene drove a well-dressed gent in a Model T Ford.

"Are you Mr Simonson?", he asked.

"Ya, I'm one of 'em," replied Zack.

"I am here to collect your payment to International Harvester."

"Well, what ya know about that." Zack was not too excited.

"I am here to get the money or take possession of the thresher and engine," replied the collector in a definite tone of voice.

"Could you come back some other day?", Zack calmly suggested.

"No, I cannot run around the country at the whim of every farmer," the collector said firmly.

"Okay, you sit in your car and don't bother any of the crew. I'll soon be back."

Zack found Roy. "There is an International collector here, and he wants the money or the outfit."

"I don't think that note is due yet, is it?", Roy scratched his head.

Zack asked "You got any money on you? I got an idea."

"I have a hundred dollar bill and some ones," Roy answered.

"Go and get every bill you can from the crew. I'll soon be back."

Zack hurried away. Going past the collector's car, Zack called, "Sit tight, I'll soon take care of you."

Getting in his Graham Page car, he drove over the rise and out of sight of the visitor. There he found the two field pitchers and about three bundle haulers. Borrowing all the money they had, he went back to brother Roy. He had gathered many one and two dollar bills. The wad of money was thick but without Roy's one hundred and Zack's fifty, all of the money wouldn't have bought very much. Walking up to the collector, Zack showed the fortune of money sandwiched between a hundred dollar bill and a fifty at the bottom of the heap.

"Well here is your money, give me the note back." Reaching for the cash the collector said, "I will have to send your note from the office. I haven't got it with me."

Zack withdrew the hand with the money. "You come collecting without the note? What kind of a crook are you? Do you even work for International Harvester? If there was a cop around here, I'd have you run in. This is a big swindle you're trying to pull, but it won't work today, so get the heck out of here and we never want to see you again."

Grandpa nodded when Zack finished his yarn, "The guy was just trying for the early collection bonus."

"That's what I figured too, but the guy was so smart and pushy that I had to put him in his place."

How-To Books

Twelve members sat around the table. Before the minutes of the last meeting were opened, there was a general discussion with no topics barred. The Short Grass writers had congregated.

John mentioned that his manuscript had been turned down by the publishers because the cocaine, the spoon, the cigarette lighter and the syringe were listed as drug paraphernalia. But, how were they all used? That was the thing that the publisher could not understand. John answered that with, "I am not writing a How-To Book on drug use for kids."

Many years ago, I am not sure when it was, radio license inspectors wore blue serge suits and plug hats. Popular Mechanics magazine had a How-To article on how to build a radio transmitting station.

Bill explained, in detail, the project he and his twelve-year-old buddy produced, from start to finish.

We found the plan in Popular Mechanics. It called for thirty-two deep glass jars. A certain brand of pickles came in a jar about two inches across and ten inches deep. We found a few at our homes, but we had to go to the Blairmore (Alberta) town dump to find enough. These jars were put into a wooden box that had a leather handle on each end. Our fathers worked at the coal mine so we were no strangers at the mine shop or the tipple. That is where we got the copper and zinc strips and acid to make our battery. The rest of the stuff we got through a mail order catalogue that came from a company that must have made a fortune off of junior scientists.

We ran our radio station from my bedroom. We read parts of the newspaper and told funny jokes. To give our listeners more variety we moved to Harry's house. They had a Victrola, so we could play music as well as news. There, it was my job to crank the Victrola.

This after school radio station was on the air for a few weeks when the commercial bug bit. Harry and I were at the hardware store to sell advertising on our radio station. The man with the blue serge suit and plug hat was talking to the store keeper.

"The signal from the unlicensed radio station seems to come from the northwest part of town. They're all family residences over there. Would you know anything about it?"

"Never heard of it myself," answered the man behind the counter.

"Has anyone bought a group of batteries lately?"

"No, not from this store."

While we listened to the questions and answers, we put our sales plan on ice. Late that night we moved our transmitter to the roof of the hotel. The next afternoon we used our secret passage to the flat roof and gave the news broadcast. We had to find out about radio laws, and keep an eye on the stranger with the plug hat. Our 'on air' time was shortened considerably. We had nearly run out of new places to move our business to. Early one morning, we were moving the battery to a new location. Right at the main street intersection we were face to face with the stranger and his plug hat. The big guy looked at our battery in disbelief.

"That is a powerful battery you boys have. I bet that it would be strong enough to run a radio station." He seemed to be talking to himself.

The big man in the blue suit was very friendly, "Yes boys, that has enough power to run an illegal transmitter. That would be bad. To have a radio station without a permit would lead to a very costly fine and possibly a long jail term."

He sure had his eye on the pickle jars. We put the lids on when we moved. All of the wire and metal strips that were soldered to it were all coiled up on top of the jars.

The stranger said, "I am a radio license inspector, and I know all about those things. But if there was no battery to operate a station, the government wouldn't have a case. I suppose you boys are going to the town dump with those pickle jars?"

"Oh yes," Harry and I said together. We each took a handle and lugged our stuff to the dump.

We learned that the inspector got on the east bound train at noon that day.

Remembering Bill's story, I wholly agree with John. A How-To Book in the wrong hands could lead to a fine, jail, or addiction.

Knot-Head Mare

I was driving six horses on a two furrow plow. Uncle Ted was driving the same size outfit, but his horses weighed more, and showed a lot more education. There were three horses side by side, with the pole of the plow between the right and center horses. The right hand horse walked in the furrow made on the last round. The other two walked in the weeds on the unplowed ground. The three in front of them were hitched in a like pattern.

My leaders (the three horses in front) were Sharp, a dappled gray mare, Roy, a dark bay gelding, and Cactus, a light bay gelding.

Uncle Ted always had a Cactus in his horse herd. Working around Cactus, you always had to be aware of the thorns.

Uncle had stopped at the corner of the triangular field, where we had our drinking water, kerosine and fly repellant. His team was resting and occasionally switching their tails at the flies.

I was approaching the rest stop when Cactus exploded. I could see most of his belly even with Roy's back every time he jumped. Cactus' five team mates got into the act real quick. We turned over that black soil in a hurry for a few hundred yards. I was able to stop them before we reached the other plow outfit.

"It's the horse flies that are bothering your team," Uncle Ted explained. He took the old gallon paint pail, with sort of a witches brew fly repellent, and the stick with the rag padded on the end to the front of my team. While I held the head of each horse, Uncle dabbed the fly stuff on their legs and bellies. That done, he returned the pail to its usual place.

"That Cactus is a knot head that looks much like a mare I rode for Jack Wallace in 1931." Uncle Ted was a young man at that time. Five foot nine inches tall, but his John B. Stetson hat made him look taller.

While I cleaned the moldboard of my plow with a kerosine rag, Uncle told his story.

It was in the dead of winter when we caught the bay mare. She had a blaze face and four white stockings just like this Cactus jug-head. We got my saddle on her and used a saddle horse on each side to get her out to the hay meadow that had deep snow on it. After we got her blindfolded, I got on and Ronald pulled off the sack we used for a blindfold. I had one whale of a ride. If she had not been handicapped by the deep snow I might not have been able to ride her. That horse was ringing wet with sweat and still bucking. That animal was one of those that you couldn't kill with hard work. The next day it was the same thing all over again, but she didn't buck so long. In about three days, I took her for a long ride. We had the cattle near home on the south side of the river. The sheep were out on the north side, in the hills. I took some grub and news papers out to the sheep herder. On a side hill north of the river, the horse slipped and fell with me. I got a really bad jolt in my back. I held onto the horse and got back on. I got to the sheep, pretty sore and stiff. The herder put my horse in a little shed he had. I stretched out on his bunk. About four o'clock the sun was going down with a big bright sun dog on each side. It was colder than blue blazes, but I had to start for home. The sheep man helped me get mounted, and I set out to the south.

Fourteen miles from the ranch buildings, I had to open a gate. I was too stiff to get back on the horse and she was jumping around too much. It was then that I knew that I should have left the gate open when I went through the first time. I was in no shape to walk those fourteen miles, so it was a case of ride or freeze to death.

I cut off one of my saddle strings and tied it around the right fetlock of the mare. Then I put the loop of my lariat rope on the other leg. I ran the rope through both stirrups and the saddle string on the right foot. I tied the end of my rope to the bottom of the gate post. When I pretended to mount, the horse went bananas. I let her go. When she hit the end of the rope, her front feet got pulled up to the stirrups. Three times she did that. I untied my rope from the post, and she stood while I got on. After a few careful steps, the rope came off the left leg, through the stirrups and caught in the saddle string. That rope on her foot was enough to keep her mind off more mischief.

I rode right up to the ranch house door and yelled until they came out and lifted me off the horse. Mrs. Wallace put a scoop of grain in a bag and sewed the end shut. The bag was put in the oven until it was hot, then I layed down on it.

A few days later, when my back was somewhat better, I went out to ride the knot-head mare again. I let my lariat rope dangle down on her leg and she stood perfectly still while I got on.

Before Uncle Ted went back to his plow seat he observed, "A person needs a Cactus horse around the place. He adds spark to a dull life."

Bad Money

Uncle Andy told me so, but I only half believed. "Gambled money is bad. If you lose much it is a hardship, if you win much it is a hardship for the loser, and the money brings you bad luck." He continued, "A guy I knew in North Dakota, took a load of wheat to town. He lost the grain cheque, team, and sleigh, all in a poker game. The next morning he caught a ride part way home with a neighbour and walked the rest of the way."

That, I agreed, was a hardship.

"One of the winning guys in that game bought himself a Winchester Shot Gun. A 12-gauge repeating pump action. He had always wanted one, and with the easy money he bought it. The day he tried it out, he shot his right foot half off."

That I agreed was bad luck.

I stayed with Aunt Edna, Uncle Andy and Cousin Irene for two years of high school. I was six weeks late getting back to school that fall. It was war time and I had just spent some time pitching sheaves into a thrashing machine. Then it took time to get my muscles in shape to sit comfortably in the ink stained maple desk.

Saturday morning I was on my way to the post office. I had just closed the front gate, and turned to main street when Donald Burton slid his Maroon Chev sedan to a stop.

"Say, can you ride for us for a couple of days? I phoned Kane's last night. They are finished with the beef round up. We can get the horses on Monday."

"I should get one of my boots sewed up?" was my only worry.

"Well, hustle. I'll get groceries and pick you up. Have you got your saddle here?"

I indicated that it was in the shed beside the garage. With no more ado, he made a U-turn and was gone.

The horses that Donald had mentioned were an assorted band of unbroken, work type horses that he and my cousin Arling had bargained for earlier in the fall. The plan was to get them north to sell for bush horses in the lumber camps.

Bill Tillet's Harness Shop was busy. George Rear said it would be all right to leave the patching on his halters while Bill sewed my problem. I paid the dime for the repair job, grabbed my boots and rushed homeward.

I was thinking to myself, "I sure made a mistake when I had these boots made so tight fitting." I had to wear the thinnest wool socks. "Prince of Wales" stockings, they were called by the old time cowboys in Alberta.

Donald and I arrived at the farm while Woodrow was tying his saddle horse in the barn. He had just ridden in from Newton's A-N ranch situated on the north horizon. He was Arling's younger brother. He and I were to be the riders. Donald and Arling were what you would call owner riders. To get the job started we were to get three saddle horses to the pasture west of Val Marie, Saskatchewan.

Donald's wife Eva, had the table loaded with fried chicken. When Mrs. Burton fried a chicken, she must have always picked one with six legs. That is how many drumsticks there were on the platter. "Eat plenty," she kept urging us. "You boys don't know when you will get to eat again."

After dinner, Woodrow and I each saddled a horse. He had his black mare Nitero, a horse that would do anything you asked of her. I was to use Pat, a blaze faced, bay gelding. He was not a show ring animal, but he could get you over a lot of ground with little effort on his part. He was a good stock horse too. Black Beauty was a mare without one white hair. We led her along for Donald to use on Monday.

Our trail angled southwest, across Tom Wood's Durham wheat stubble, through the willows at Mosquito Creek and over the abandoned sand plain with its deep blow holes. Night overtook us northeast of Ponteix. When it got dark that night, it got real dark. We couldn't see our horses' ears. But, thank goodness for their big eyes, they kept on the road.

As we neared town, the low clouds thinned and we had enough moonlight to get our mounts and Beauty taken care of at the Thibodeau farm. We walked the one half mile into town to the Chinese Café. Pork

19

chops, potatoes and apple pie sure hit the spot. This kind gentleman also had rooms upstairs, so with a promise of breakfast at 6:00 a.m., we went to bed. In the middle of the night I woke up with my cheeks smarting.

This old guy has washed these pillow cases in lye water and not rinsed them enough. I sleepily pushed the pillow onto the floor and went back to sleep. At 6 a.m., there was breakfast on a table in the dining room. When I appeared our host took one look at me and he said. "Boy, you got bad wind burn. Have you been cowboying in jail?" The old oriental chuckled at his own joke. Shortly, he returned to our table with a teaspoon of strange ointment.

"Put this on the red spots," he said as he returned to the kitchen. Without a mirror, how could I tell where the red spots were? I put the stuff on the sore spots. It was strange ointment. I felt better right away. Now, I would guess that it was Aloe Vera sap and some Chinese herb mixed together. Anyway, it sure did work.

We rode through Ponteix before daylight. The temperature was warm for that time of day. Travelling straight south for a few miles, we came to unfenced land. Then we could beeline to Brazzer's ranch south of Cadillac. At the door of their house, Phil Brazzer, short, heavy-set and chewing on a toothpick, greeted us.

"Put your horses in the barn and feed them. Florence will have some thing ready for you."

We ate heartily and hit the saddles. There were still miles to go. Sunset found us on the high rolling land above the White Mud valley. There were snow drifts in the coulees. This was more evident the farther south we went. Our parkas were untied from the saddles and put on. As we descended to the valley floor, it got dark. Moving west on the trail, we rode into the moonrise of the century. It must have been fog in the valley that had turned to ice crystals that gave us the feeling that we were riding into a huge amphitheatre. Visibility was about fifty yards to the sides and above. The moonlight shining over our shoulders gave a silver blue look to the world around us. Looking back, we saw countless faint little blue sparkles in the air.

"Come on let's push along. If we are being chased by fairies we better get a move on," was Woodrow's idea.

I had to agree, so we sped up the pace for a couple of miles. Arriving at the P.F.R.A. headquarters, we and our horses were fed and sheltered. At the bunkhouse there were two of the range crew and five construction people. They welcomed us.

"New money! You guys are just what we have been waiting for. The game is low card rap, a nickel a rap, a dime a set." This invitation and warning were given by a carpenter.

Woodrow declined. I said, "I still have thirty-five cents of my threshing wages. I will donate that to the cause."

I got the rusty cream can padded with an old coat to sit on. The table must have suffered four leg amputations as it was lower than a normal piece of furniture. The first deal, I got a hand of small numbered cards. I rapped my knuckles on the table to signal that I figured I had a winning hand. I did win, and I did again and again. When the game broke up at bed time I still had my thirty-five cents plus another four dollars.

I don't remember what the hitch was, but we didn't chase horses on Monday. Arling and Donald picked Woodrow and me up and we had dinner in the Val Marie Hotel. Crossing the street to a store, I found lined horse hide roper gloves for less than four dollars. I tried a pair on and they fit so well and felt so nice that I loathed taking one off to dig out the money to pay for them. I threw my old gloves away. I spent a lot of time bragging about my new warm gloves which meant that I opened every bloody gate we drove through the rest of the day.

Tuesday we chased horses. Arling left, driving his Plymouth. Donald left, riding Black Beauty. He had different directions to the pasture up north where the forty head of bush horses were being held. Woodrow and I, with the help of one of the men, chased seven head of Thoroughbred mares east up the trail we had come in on. At a deep coulee, he told us to follow it until we gained the bench land, then head past the next three coulees and turn north. There you will find the gate into the other pasture.

The more miles that we followed this coulee, the deeper the snow was. We were about a quarter of a mile from the north end, when our band of racy-type mares went up the east bank and turned back toward their old home. This meant serious riding for us. We did not

21

head the next three coulees, we crossed them. The snow was powder on the west bank of the coulees and the mares and Nitreo made their own snow storm in each one they crossed.

Through the third coulee we were out on level ground. Off to the north were the fence and gate that we had to go through. Woodrow had the horses running in a curve that would get to the fence. All was well there, so I went to open the gate where the snow was knee deep with a crust.

I led Pat away from the gate to a spot that would encourage our little band to go where we wanted them. It was time to tighten my cinch. You can't handle thin latigo with gloves on. I put mine in my chaps pocket. By the time I had my cinch snugged up, Woodrow and the stock were heading north. All I had to do was close the gate and catch up. Pat just wanted to catch up. He thought 'to heck with the gate.' We danced around in the snowbank until it was pretty well plowed up. That bay horse was unruly. With the gate closed and mounted up, I reached for my gloves. The left-hand glove was all that I had left. Looking at the big circle of chewed up snowbank, and knowing my glove was in there somewhere, was disheartening.

I saw Woodrow and the horses going out of sight a mile away. Pat made the decision as to whether or not we would look for a glove in the snowbank (like a needle in a haystack). With two crow hop jumps, he was turned north. I settled in my saddle and let him go.

We joined the big herd and moved them to Cadillac to be shipped by rail. The only time that afternoon that my right hand was warm, was when we grazed the stock in a sheltered creek bottom for an hour. The next day Arling, Woodrow and I chased the seven Thoroughbred mares to Donald's farm, north of Vanguard. Let me tell you, it was chilly. And with no glove on my right hand, I was either breathing on it, sitting on it, scratching my arm pit with it, or any thing else to keep it warm.

The first day back in school was like any other, class dismissed, take our books home and pile in the porch. Then hurry to the pool room to keep up with local talk.

They had a rap poker game going. The stakes were one cent or two if you got caught. I had eight pennies. I got in the game. Later, Leonard that lived around the corner from us and wore knee-laced engineer's boots, thought that we should go home to eat. It was nearly six bells. Gathering up my winnings, we left the poolroom.

"Hey, just a minute. I have enough money here to buy toothpaste, and here is the store." Len followed me in.

Len would have to clown around with my Colgate box. It was in such bad shape that Ethel-May garbaged it and put the tube of toothpaste in a paper bag. Len was the shortest guy in class but always took long steps. When he got those high-laced boots moving, they sure went. We had taken a few steps down the sidewalk, when my toothpaste tube cut through the bag and landed on the very same spot that Len's boot did, only a half instant sooner. The boot came down and up went a white rainbow of tooth paste.

I picked up the squashed, empty toothpaste tube and flipped it into the weeds on the vacant lot and said, "Son-of-a-gun, Uncle Andy is right." I recalled the poker game in North Dakota that he told be about where one guy lost his grain cheque, team and sleigh and the other guy lost his foot from his new shot gun. Then I thought to myself, "Good thing tooth paste couldn't blow a foot off!"

23

Luck, Plus Or Minus

Denver, Colorado appeared to be a fifty-mile long string of oncoming car lights. The stress came at the outskirts of the city. The rain that fell in the predawn hours had frozen to the highway. Semi rigs were lying on their sides. Blue and brown 4x4's were in the ditch. A little red car sat in a meridian strip with its hood folded on its roof. The rain had turned to snow that fell in large wet flakes. Driving required complete attention.

Cheyenne, Wyoming seemed a long way off. Reaching there, we learned that the road leading northwest was snowed in too. Not to be weather bound, we travelled northeast. Driving for hours, the only visible association with reality was the odd road sign. The road was still bad. The snow still fell.

At sunset we come to dry pavement. That was something we had not seen in ten hours of travel. Strange, too, that it would be at the very edge of the Black Hills of South Dakota that we found good weather.

Registering at the majestic Franklin House of Deadwood, with its bygone charm, we could lay down and shut our eyes. After retiring, it took a short time for the sight of large snowflakes showing through closed eyelids to give way to sleep.

Dawn was picture postcard perfect, but a foot of clean white snow had fallen. A fast thaw was predicted, so we stayed for the morning. The casinos beckoned, so I lost a couple of bucks trying to win a new Ford car.

The streets were awash with melting snow. We checked out of the hotel, had a lunch and were ready to move on through Montana and get home. At the lunch counter till, the girl gave me three quarters in my change. To my travelling companion I said, "You know, Berniece, I'm going down the street three doors, and buy that Red Ford for seventy-five cents."

At the slot machine I dropped in the three coins. I pressed the spin button. The first time around I got three bars. Now that was thirty quarters or that many credits. I was after the car. I pressed the button that said play full credits, then the spin tab. That used up three credits (or quarters), and I got nothing.

To win the car you had to play three tokens at a time. You also had to get the red white and blue seven on the pay line. I pressed the play and spin tabs again. The wheels whirled and on the left, the red seven stopped right on the line. The white seven stopped on the line. To the right, the wheel slowed and the blue seven stopped one speck short of the line. My loss was there to see.

I understand the US IRS would charge me a tax on a win like that. I know that our combined governments would cost me 16 percent. Would they charge me on the seventy-five cents, that being my cost, or would they use the $25,000 price of the car?

I will never know!

Travelling in Montana

We were still in Canada. It was along the Red Rock Canyon trail in Waterton Park, that we met them. Sharing the scenery with this couple of tourists, it had to follow that we struck up a conversation.

"By your license plate I can see that you folks are Canadian," was his observation.

"Yes, we live in Saskatchewan," I replied. "Where are you folks from."

"We are from Saint Louis, Missouri". "We flew into Great Falls and got a you-drive," the lady continued. "We drove to Cardston last night and stayed in a motel. It was such a nice room and reasonable too."

"I wonder how it will be to get a room in Montana tonight?" was my question.

"You will have no problem at all. In the states there are motels all over the place. Anywhere you want to look."

"Well, thank you. That makes us feel confident." The park took our attention, but the conversation still flowed free and easy.

"What is it like in your part of the world?" the American asked.

"We are from a small town on the edge of the agricultural areas. North of us, a few miles, is the northern forest. We have twenty-five lakes within twenty-five miles of town. If you would care for a feed of fresh fish come and join us."

"Sounds great," said the Missourian. "I was in the red meat industry and I can still do the best barbecued steak you could ever eat. When you are in our part of the country, be sure to look us up. I mean that." He said.

Berniece said, "It sounds so delicious I think that we will stop in at your house."

"Thanks for the visit. It has been nice. Bye now," was the reply.

"Enjoy your stay in Canada. Good Bye," I added.

Hours later, we missed a highway sign. No problem! We were still going the right direction, until there was a fork in the trail. Now what? We turned right. I didn't know where we were going and in the next four miles the road gave us the impression that it didn't know where it was going either. It went every direction imaginable, it did everything but cross itself.

The parking lot at the foot of the mountain had two cars parked in it. While we were pouring over the road map, a couple emerged from the forest foot path. They had driven on every trail nearby in the last two days, and now were going to Canada. The next half hour was consumed by pleasant visiting. He was a lawyer in Boston, she managed their sea side home. On parting she, with a mischievous yet sincere grin, said, "If you ever get lost in Boston's Back Bay area, stop at our house for a cup of tea."

"Do you mean that after the Boston Teaparty, tea is still the favourite drink?"

"I can make coffee too, come anyway. Bye, bye."

"Thank You and Goodbye."

In the afternoon, on the tour boat on the mountain lake, we talked to the couple across from us. At the end of the trip we were invited thus, "Please stop in at West Yellowstone, but if you come this week end we may have to throw some relatives out to make room at the table."

"Thanks and Goodbye."

A bit more driving and we were out of the mountains and cruising along in the valley.

"Let's get a motel first, then have our evening meal," Berniece suggested.

The next town had no vacancies. I drove faster to the next town, no vacancies. The sun had set. There, beside the road, was a large three story hotel on the right. I turned in. The sign on the door read 'CLOSED'. As we regained the pavement, I looked in the mirror and a parade of cars were behind us, all with their signal lights indicating a right turn. There were dozens of people looking for a place to sleep. Missouri, Boston, West Yellowstone, all out of reach this evening. We had begin to feel like lost orphans.

At Polsen, Montana I said, "This is it. Let's see if we can get a reservation for some place down the road."

Stopping at the first motel, we learned that there was not one available bed in western Montana.

"But I have a friend who may be able to help you," said the desk clerk.

A quick phone call and we were directed to main street and the Wolf's Den Bar.

"We usually rent out the suite in the back on week ends only. But if you wish, we could make it up in a few minutes," said the proprietor.

The patrons of the bar were very considerate. It was quiet and we had a good night's sleep. The coffee we enjoyed with the pretty barmaid the next morning was delicious.

An Actor?

You would expect rain and fog in the mountain valleys at that time of year. There was no traffic to speak of. The only tie with civilization was the center line of the highway. What I did not expect was the tramp beside the road.

His fur and leather clothes looked to be at least one hundred years old. On a night like that, I could not pass up a poor human alone, on foot, so far away from shelter. I stopped, leaned over and opened the passenger's door. There he stood, quite and dumbfounded.

"Come out of the rain," I invited.

The gent, very gingerly, sat in the car. His movements and attitude were like mine would be, if I were invited to step into an interplanetary craft run by purple people.

"Where do you wish to go?" I asked.

"I dina know. I have no encountered my party that were on the water."

"Do you mean the Thompson river?"

"Noo, noo. It would have no name. It was discovered only a fort night past."

"If you were on a river, it has to be the Thompson."

"Weel, my party ere to come up the stream with two canoes while I explore on foot."

"Where would you meet if you were separated?"

"The Gentlemen Adventurers will soon build a post made on water to Hudson's Bay. Aye, the talk was it would have the name of Edmonton, like the glory of the highlands. There I would wait for them, but without pemmican and no victuals at hand, it would be a bad expedition."

My plan was to stop a the first motel that I came to. That all changed with the odour of my passenger.

"What kind of a chariot conveyance is this?" my passenger asked.

"It is a Chevrolet."

29

"Chevrolet! This would be a French device?"

"No, it was made in Canada."

"Upper, or Lower Canada?"

"Oshawa. I guess it would be Upper Canada."

"Ye gravitate doon hill but how do ye get uphill without animal beasts or river men?"

That question was easy, "It has an internal combustion engine," I answered.

"Infernal combustion," he paused, "that sounds Papist to me. I be within the flock of Scot Presbyterian."

I would have liked to ask when he had last taken a bath. "How long have you been away from home?"

"Home, in York Factor, is three seasons away. It has taken months to cross the mountains."

"Were you at the BC coast?"

"Do ye be dense? 'BC coast', what is that? We set oot to find the track overland to the great salt water."

"Did you find it?" I humbly asked.

"Ye are dense. I am here, am I not?"

"Have you anything to show that you were at the ocean?"

"Aye, with powdered stone and bear grease I wrote, 'ALEXANDER MACKENZIE FROM CANADA BY LAND 22 OF JULY 1793' on a sheltered side of the cliff."

I cut off the heater and went for air conditioning, even opened the windows. This old boy had an odour. My new found friend went to sleep. He sure did have his part down pat.

Miles later, we stopped at the West Edmonton Mall. The glare of the lights woke Alexander Mackenzie up.

"When did you set out to re-enact this pageant?"

"Pageant? Pageant I noo ken understand ye." He kept turning his head like a sitting duck that was buckshot shy.

I reached over, unlatched his door and pointed to the entrance to the mall, "You will find it all in there." The woebegone old duck waddled in the right direction.

Later that day, in the car, I found a small brass coin or disc, with strange words around the edge. In the center was the old Hudson's Bay mark. This, and a small scrap of leather from his ragged coat, must have been lost by the man from the explorer's pageant.

I sent the coin to the Bay Archives in Winnipeg. They, in time, assured me that it was an authentic HBC trade token. Very few had been cast and the one that I had sent was, by far, in the most new condition that they had seen. They were mailing it back to me.

Then the scrap of leather, it went to Canada Research. Their response was as follows:

Dear Sir:

The exhaustive tests on the specimen you submitted prove, without a doubt, that the leather was tanned in Scotland on June 14, 1789.

We deeply regret that, due to the age and fragility of the small sample that you submitted, while undergoing testing it disintegrated.

Yours

Truly ---

I phoned the Bay Archives. They had returned the token by mail. There was a receipt, but it was not insured and it seemed that Canada Post had lost it.

The only thing I can do is forget the whole thing. Without proof, no one would believe that I gave Alex Mackenzie a lift. In fact, I don't believe it myself.

The Parade

Summer was on its way. The crops were growing, not as good as some I remembered, but growing never-the-less.

Most of the soldiers had returned home. Some to only stop for a day or two then went on to conquer their own piece of the planet.

It was not an official meeting, a group of local supporters had gathered at the Oddfellows hall to plan a day of celebration.

The sun was setting through a thin veil of dust. The threat of drought hung over the countryside. It was a gloomy evening.

For this meeting there was no recording secretary so therefore, no minutes. The guys just sat around and pondered. "What to do for a sports day this summer?"

The rodeo grounds were in a shambles. Many corral rails were broken or missing. The chutes were in disrepair. Money to rebuild was not available. That meant that a rodeo was out of the question.

Baseball! Everyone loved baseball. We could not field a team ourselves this season. Most, if not all, small prairie towns had to live without a baseball team. Even if a large amount of cash could be found for prize money, there would still not be enough teams to make it a day like in years gone by.

"It is a crime the way things are going. It was easier to have a good time back in the hard time years of the thirty's, than it is now," just a random thought from one of the group.

"Say how about a day of horse racing?"

"No, there aren't any race horses left in the country and if there were, money would be the problem there too."

"Times have changed, and not for the better, as far as our town is concerned."

"I suppose, if we had a parade no one would put in a float, and if they did no one would come out to see it."

"Maybe we would have to have a Lady Godiva to lead our parade."

Joe was of the intellectual type, medium height, becoming slightly rounded and what hair he had left was gray. His life was devoted to bachelorhood. Not a word had he uttered since the original "Hello," but the last idea mentioned just made his blue eyes sparkle. His whole body was alive. He showed the only real enthusiasm of the gathered people.

"We have to have Lady Godiva. I haven't seen a good white horse since I left Ireland!"

Grandma Maria

Maria was an honest to goodness pioneer lady. A long, long time ago, two brothers left Northern Germany to live in the American Colonies. One of these hardy souls was Grandma Maria's ancestor. As time went on the descendants of the two guys spread over a lot of country. I was really taken by her granddaughter. In fact, in a short while, she and I will have been married for fifty years.

When a family has grown for a couple of hundred years, it is rather hard to put the lineage down without using reams of paper.

Great Great Great Grandpa was ranching in a valley in Oregon. On a Saturday evening he was in the local saloon, minding his own business, and enjoying a drink. A young patron thought that he would have some fun with the old guy. Rude remarks turned to insults. They turned to shadow boxing. The lad was just getting into things when the bar keeper and the bouncer took the self-styled comedian each by an arm. His toes did not touch the floor until he was at the door.

"Aw, come on fellas, I was just having fun with the old guy," the sport complained.

The bar keeper answered, "See that black handled Colt 45 tucked in his belt? Well, he signalled us that he was just about ready to use it like he did on the last green horn kid that bothered him."

The grandpa's granddaddy was moving a small heard of cattle through a mountain pass when he was stopped by Indians. They were hungry and seeing that the white men had stolen their buffalo, they stole the cattle and had something to eat.

When he was found, his rifle and both side arms were empty. He must have gotten off about twenty shots before he went down, but he was so full of arrows that he was like a pin cushion. That fella would be a Great Great Great Great Great Grandfather.

I am not a person that can take a new command very gracefully, especially when I have pressing business up town.

"Those eave trough leaks just have to be fixed," my wife suggested.

"Yes, I'll do that one of these days."

"They are forecasting rain for later today."

"When I get back from up town, I suppose I could look at them."

"Yes, and by that time it will be raining."

"What is the big rush this morning? The eaves troughs have been like that for over a year."

"Yes, and every time it rains, it washes holes in my flower bed."

"The guys will be at the coffee shop up town, right now."

"The eaves troughs should be fixed right now."

"But darn it all woman, I don't wan...."

Then I remembered Grandpa to the third power and even the one with five greats, and I had been arguing with their girl!

"Yes, dear," and I went to get the ladder.

The Last Bite

Winter 1943. Canada was at war with Germany, Italy, and Japan. Many local young men and some young women as well, were in the armed forces. Some of them where at the front lines in the thick of the conflict. Others had not progressed that far, but were in training camps. The safety of these people hung like a mantel of grey over our community as it did for every other part of the nation. When he went to war, Wing Lee left the Crown Café and his Irish Setter in care of his aged partner Cook Quan.

The big, red bird dog was also called Wing. To while away the months, Wing visited nearly every home in town. Where he felt totally welcome, he would come right in. If he had only a nodding acquaintance, he may just lie on the front step for a while.

For us school students, there was no great hardship involved, but many regular items that we had taken for granted were in short supply. Gasoline, antifreeze, tires, all sugars, butter, silk hose, and the list went on. To us teenagers, life was great. Maybe next year would find us over there, but for the time being, we were living in the here and now.

To find the time to do homework was a problem. A larger problem was the show at the Royal Theatre. The same picture was shown Friday and Saturday nights. If you did not see the show on Friday night, you had to be a recluse all day Saturday. If you mingled, every kid in town would tell you every last little detail of the last night's show. Going to the movie on Friday left us at loose ends on Saturday night.

Saturday night was Bridge Club get-together. It was a small club, four couples. Uncle Andy and Aunt Edna, whom I stayed with during my high school years, were the hosts on this Saturday night. Mr. and Mrs. Fairburn were the first to arrive. I said "Hello," then I was on my way up the street. While my uncle took care of their coats, Mrs. Fairburn told Aunt Edna of her good fortune.

"Tomorrow afternoon, I host the church ladies in our war effort group. I will have enough tea to serve them. I had just enough sugar and butter to make donuts. It worked out so neatly, two donuts for each person. I used up all of our sugar ration coupons. There will be no sugar at our house until next month's coupons become valid."

At the pool room I found Sid Fairburn, a school crony. After a lengthy visit with John Secar, the pool hall attendant, we wandered across the street to the café. Cook sat behind the counter reading his newspaper that had the strange characters running up and down the page. He was all alone. After a visit with us, and as we were just killing time, the newspaper turned out to be more interesting to him than Sid and I were. Cook went back to reading. We went to the curling rink. Wing followed us. The rink was dark and locked. The hotel bar was out of bounds for seventeen year olds. We had been to the theatre on Friday night. The only hangouts for us were the pool room or the café. We had done that route. Sid figured we might as well go to his home. Wing and I followed him up the stairs to their apartment above the Royal Bank. In Sid's room we whiled away the time with his books and things. This was not a wild roaring Saturday night, just a relaxing night.

"There must be something to eat around here."

When Sid said this, it was the cue for Wing and I to join him in the kitchen.

Wing stretched out on a scatter rug. I took a chair at the table. Two tumblers and a glass bottle of cold milk were on the table. But things took a fast turn for the better when my pal marched out of the pantry with the air of a great chef, carrying a pyramid of donuts on a large platter. Now we were into good food, rich, crunchy, tasty, Umm, good!

"Have another one."

"Thanks, don't mind if I do."

"Another glass of milk? We still have lots of donuts."

"Okay, they sure do taste good."

Then there came the problem. How to get the milk to last as long as the donuts. Geometry was not applicable, nor was algebra. After enough clowny ideas, we counted the donuts, divided the milk into our glasses, then used the English pub system of so many fingers. It worked out quite well. There was one donut left in the middle of that great big plate. Right then, Wing gave out with a dog yawn. We tossed the last golden treat to the dog.

The witching hour had passed so we started home. Wing dropped off at the café and I went on home alone. As I came in, the Fairburns were about to leave.

"We left you one sandwich," Mr Fairburn said, pointing to the table.

"Thanks. That's better than I did. There was one donut left but we fed that to the Chinaman's dog."

My aunt told me later why Mrs. Fairburn turned quite pale and had such a shook up look. Sunday morning my Aunt appointed me, as a committee of one, to canvas at the houses of VanWarmer's and Ritchie's for donations of sugar. We had scads of butter that my Mom kept sending from the farm. Mrs. Fairburn was able to make a small chocolate cake in a rush.

The Good Life

"Yes sir, I'd go back tomorrow if I could. That was the best way a fella could live in those days," Tom said, as he rested his elbows on the patio table. Tom and I were sitting on the veranda of his home in Lethbridge, Alberta. As the traffic sped by on Eleventh Avenue, he continued.

"It was easy clean work, just a few hundred head of cattle and the line camp to look after. We were out many miles west of the home ranch. I was sixteen years old the first time that I worked line camp. I was with Shorty Merrino that fall. He was a little bit of a Mexican, but what he did not know about horses or cattle was not worth knowing."

I interrupted, "I remember hearing of that guy being in Saskatchewan at the turn of the century. I wonder whatever happened to him?"I mused. Tom grinned, "Everything that could happen to a cowboy, storms, wild horses, wilder cows, the whole works, but never a saddle sore. He was so warped and twisted that he fit a saddle perfect. There was no part of him that took any more wear than any other spot."

I corrected myself, "No I meant how long did he last?"

"Forever," Tom replied. "A month ago I was in the alignment pit doing a Mercury. I noticed this guy with the biggest black hat you ever saw, standing watching me. The hat was as big as he was. He was suntanned, white hair, and sparkling brown eyes. I got out of the pit and shook hands and said, "Shorty how in the heck are you?" He just beamed and said, 'I can't run very fast but I'm sure full of knowledge.'" Tom went on, "He is more than eighty years old and still holed up on some ranch along the Montana border."

"I started riding at the line camp with Shorty the first year that I worked on that ranch. One day we were out at the far southwest corner of the pasture. The sun was bright and warm. We finished checking a deep coulee to see if there were any cattle hid out there. When we climbed out onto the bench land, Shorty said, "Ride kid." With that we galloped northeast toward our cabin. The blue-black cloud from the northwest was rolling down on us. Then the air got really cold. It was

39

a storm in the Chinook country. When the snow swirled around us, Shorty slowed up. He took his lariat and dropped a loop over my horse's head, then led my horse on about ten feet of rope. That was to make sure that we did not get separated in the storm. He said that we had to save our horses because we had a long way to go. The wind was on our left side and sometimes at our back, and boy it was cold. Just after dark we rode down a very steep hill. At the bottom there were a few cottonwood trees, but mostly willows. We were so lost that we didn't even know directions. Shorty said, "We had best stay here and get a fire going." He added, "Unsaddle and let the horses go. They need a chance to look out for themselves."

While one guy tramped up and down the willow clumps for fire wood and kept a small blaze going, the other would try to rest under the saddle pads. It was a bad storm, you could not see a hand in front of your face if you got away from the trees. It lasted that night, and the next day and night. About an hour before daylight the wind went down. Boy oh boy, we were nearly starved, nothing to eat since the day before yesterday. When it did get light, we looked down and there were our horses, eating at the haystack. We had camped out four hundred yards from our cabin."

Tom said, "Sit still while I get some refreshments." I sat and subconsciously counted the new 1958 Pontiacs that zipped by on the other side of the hedge. When Tom returned he went on, "The next year I was at the line camp alone. There were a hundred and eighty head of steers that I had to keep drifting east, really slow. The idea was to have them near the home place about New Years in case the weather got bad and we had to feed the critters.

In the early fall it was pretty good. There was a spring in another pasture less than ten miles away. We had a really good picnic spot in the trees. There were seven other guys and myself that would meet there every Wednesday night. We kept a big old granite coffee pot there, with tin cups. We would sit half the night and drink coffee and tell stories. Everyone had one week to make up a bigger lie or funnier yarn than was told that night.

It got too cold for our outside get togethers. Then it got to be a bit on the lonesome side. One night I opened the trap door to the attic.

There I found the next thing to a gold mine. There were piles of old wild west magazines and old news papers. When you are all alone for weeks on end, it sure is nice to have something to read in the evening.

I took down a few things, and left the door open. I had planed on crawling up there again in the morning. I darn near lost the cabin that morning but I did save it. I used to get up about six o'clock, light the fire, and go back to bed for an hour. I was half-dozed off when, up in the attic, I saw a flicker of light. Holy cats! There was a paper that got pushed against the stove pipe and it caught fire. I pulled on my boots and mackinaw, grabbed the water pail and ran out to the well. I hooked the pail on the rope and dropped it down the well. Clunk. The well was frozen over. It would be a two day ride to call in a fire truck, then it would have had to come in a hundred miles.

When you are standing in your long underwear and coat and boots, and the well is iced over and your house is on fire, that is LONESOME!"

The Watch Dog

I was 19 when I met Berniece Doll. During the summer, we saw each other at a few dances, at the Elks Hall. Vivian, a neighbour's daughter, was enrolled at Hodgeville High. We discovered we had a friend in common, her roommate Berniece.

Through the winter I did ride into town a few times and take this nice girl to a show. A late January thaw lasted two days, resulted in a lot of ice. I had to shoe my saddle horse for safety sake, and to make better time on the icy trail. Of course, I stopped at the girls' suite every chance I got. It was a long cold winter or I may have worn out my welcome. A couple of weeks after Easter, the snow was on its way to Old Wives Lake. The roads dried up so a car was usable, my horse must have felt semi-retired.

Step one - inflate tires, step two - get the motor running, step three - find and fix the loose coil wire. That was enough steps, it was Saturday morning. With a bit of dusting and cleaning, and a red woolen blanket over the somewhat shabby seat in the Chevy, I felt that it was ready to go.

On Saturday evening I headed east. I was running on teenage bravery, and I quaked at the thought of meeting HER parents. I had met a sister and three brothers, but not her parents or a younger brother and sister. When I stopped in front of Mr. Doll's house, and timidly stepped out of the car, I was met by Jerry. After a friendly hello, he pointed to the black and white collie dog laying right across the doorway.

"Do you know Max?" he asked. I admitted that I had heard of him. He continued, "The teacher stayed here before her and Max were married. Max never parked way out here. He would drive right up to the door step and make a jump to get in the house before the dog bit him." While I was digesting this bit of news, and eyeing the dog who seemed uninterested in me and the rest of his surroundings, Jerry went about his chores. While I was figuring out how to get around this mean beast, Berniece came out. With a friendly greeting she said, "Come in."

With a couple of hesitant steps and a fast swallow, I asked, "What about the dog?" She aimed a gentle yet firm toe at Nipper's ribs. He, in turn, slowly arose and wandered away. Then, with a smile, she assured me, "He is just a gentle old pooch." Then roguishly added, "I bet he likes you nearly as much as I do." Right then I figured that I had my foot in the door.

The Ranch Lady

Shelby has the bluest eyes, spun gold hair, and an angelic face. A prettier five year old girl would be very hard to find. Her older sister goes to school, her younger sister does not, as yet, have the freedom of the ranch yard. Grandma and Grandpa's house is only a one minute run from home.

Grandma Doris is no stranger to the corrals, but it is Grandpa Dennis and Shelby that really run the ranch. These two are not only working partners, but buddies as well. The condition of cattle, the grass land, the hay crop, and the feed and water supply are always under the eye of these two.

At weaning time for the calves, Old Hercules, the Simmental bull, was penned up waiting for a ride to market. "Why do we have to sell him, Grandpa?" asked Shelby.

"He is old and injured. He cannot be the father of any more calves."

"Couldn't we keep him and let him stay in the corral and eat hay?" Shelby did not want to part with this good old bull.

"If we keep him, he may eat up the hay that we need for the calves. And in the summer he would eat up the grass that we need for the cow herd," Grandpa advised. The young ranch lady saw the reasoning of all this, "Yup, he's got to go."

With Grandpa Dennis' coaching, this girl knew her business. She had knowledge that it would take some people half a lifetime to get. An aunt and uncle came to the ranch for a visit. They had a new baby boy to proudly show the family. The little guy, with his red face and tiny clinched fists, had his eyes shut in sleep. Shelby and her sisters were thrilled to have a new cousin. He was so sweet.

In the general conversation, adoption was mentioned. Shelby went right to the heart of things, and asked her aunt for an explanation. A lengthy discussion followed. The young ranch lady had added to her store of knowledge. Then one more question wrinkled the little brow above the blue eyes, "But if you can get babies by just signing for them at the hospital, why do you keep uncle around?"

Ownership

I had one elbow on the counter, while Ron made out the receipt for the six, five pound pails of grease in the carton.

"I sure am sorry to see you go," I said.

"Well a person has to move along with the times, that's why I sold the bulk fuel business, lock stock and barrel like they used to say. The truck goes too."

"Yes that's the way I figured when I sold the place down northwest of Mankota."

"Who did you know down in that country?" That question led to a big long visit.

"Did you ever meet Bill?", Ron asked.

"Ya, when I worked in Moose Jaw years ago. The Myers brothers had a garage, where they sold Hillman Minx cars. They also had a ranch. Bill worked at the ranch, I worked in the garage." When I gave that answer, Ron fairly beamed and he told this story.

We were coming home from a rodeo, we had stayed for the dance and it was sunrise Monday morning by the time we were close to home. There were a half a dozen spring calves laying in a hollow beside the road.

"We should rope them, and haul them into the stockyards at Moose Jaw," Bill figured.

"No we should go home and go to bed," I told him. I woke up about noon. Bill was gone. So were his lariat rope and his truck, nothing else. I knew right then, those calves were on their way to the stockyards. The cops were waiting for Bill when he came home.

It was late fall when he started serving time. After harvest I got a job that lasted into the winter, then nothing. I joined the army. It was spring before I got a leave to go and see Bill at the jail. When he first saw me, he howled.

"Where in hell did you get the monkey suit?" I looked around to see if the guard had heard this unpatriotic statement.

"Don't say that Bill. You may get in trouble. I joined the army after new years."

"They offered me freedom if I would wear one of them damn monkey suits. Guess where I told them to go! You know what I did last winter? I stole a horse while I was here in jail." Bill was proud of the feat.

He told me, "I was hauling straw with a team and hayrack. The straw pile was out north about ten miles. A guard came along to look after me. He had a buffalo coat, fur cap and big mitts. The guard just stood there while I forked on a load of straw. We got to know one another pretty well. He was a city man and not used to the outside. I refused the job unless they let me have my old buckskin jacket to wear.

As the weather got colder, so did the guard. Now, there was an old horse living on dry grass in a willow clump. My friend, the guard, could not understand how I could get by with my small jacket. I explained that was the way I had always lived, and it was not so cold. I started working on the guy, feeling so sorry for him.

"Here I'm in jail and you have to freeze, it's not right." A few days of that talk and he was getting real cold. There was a farm yard up the road, just far enough out that you could not see it from the jail.

I said, "It's not right that you have to suffer because of stupid regulations. Why don't we stop and lay our cards on the table and let them know how things are? You stay here and I'll go and get the straw and pick you up on the way home. There is no way I could escape on foot in all this snow, and I would never make it with a team and wagon. The farm couple saw it our way. I drove hard and put on a small load. When I came to the old horse, I tied a rope around his neck, took the fence down and tied him to the back end of the rack. Down the road apiece I met a fella with a team and sleigh. We stopped to rest the horses.

"Do you want to buy a horse?"

"Yes, but I can't afford one."

"How much have you got?"

"Thirty dollars."

"Give me the money, and he's yours."

47

I tied the old horse to his sleigh and went to pick up my guard. Yes sir, I stole a horse while in jail."

Ron said, "Bill was a good friend and I wouldn't want to call him a horse thief."

I had to agree, "Maybe we could say that he just readjusted the ownership of the horse."

Don't do it Lady

Bob hung up the phone, "That was Jim calling. He's in Saskatoon. We'll go in and get him first thing in the morning." Bob continued, "We'll have a real early breakfast, Dad you feed grain to the heifers and I will take a flashlight and check the calving pen. Then we will go to Saskatoon and get Jim."

"I could stay home and do up the chores," offered Eph McKellep

"No Dad, you come along. We will get Jim home and put him to work."

Bob, after years of cab driving, had learned short cuts. He parked the big, blue Dodge right against the back wall of the hotel.

"You stay with the car Dad. I'll go and get Jim and his bag."

Even though it was a frosty morning in March, Eph got out to have a stretch and stroll in the ally. A sound drew his eyes to a second story window. A feminine foot, ankle, calf and thigh slid out and over the window sill. With a mixture of sobs and grunts the other leg came into view, it was just as large as the first one. The lady got her head out of the window but not her arms and shoulders.

"Don't do it lady. Don't jump." With his big black Stetson waving in his hand, he kept up a steady line of talk. "Don't jump. You might break a leg." The old time rancher was stepping in little circles, waving his hat and talking. "You should have been there when I got a broken leg down in the corral. Let me tell you girl, that was painful. I couldn't move. It just hurt so much, all I could do was lay there and yell for help. Don't jump lady. It isn't worth the pain. If you jump, you will break a leg for sure. Maybe both legs and that would be terrible."

Things came to a head all at once. A burly pair of arms hauled the lady back into the hotel. Bob and Jim came through the side door. Eph got his black hat on and yelled to Bob and Jim "Get in the car, quick. Head for the ranch. She may try to get out the window again. If she jumped out the window, she would surely smash the Dodge!"

49

The Zane Grey Man

"When I came to Herbert years ago, people would ask me if I was related to the Black Donnleys in Ontario. Having a rather small body the size of mine, I needed every advantage I could find, so I told them that I came from the real tough Blue Ridge Donnleys of Virginia. To start a fight with one of us was like being at war with half the state, and that happened every Saturday night. We didn't like to admit even knowing that sissy bunch of pantyweights in Ontario," Ambrose explained with a smile as mischievous as a school boy.

Ambrose lived by his own code. "Do your best, do it right, and be fair to man and beast." Surveying his old machinery, which was an island of rusted iron between the barn and pasture gate, he explained, "When it won't work for me, it's not much good to anyone else. That is why I never trade in old stuff. If I made a good deal on a worn out machine, I would be buying myself an enemy."

Near the fence was the plow that turned the first sod on the homestead. At the outer edge of the collection were the red combine and swather that were field ready. Between these items one could see nearly every kind of a machine that was used in farming from the early days until now, and the location of each piece was like hen droppings in a chicken yard, just parked at random. There was no shortage of land, so this junked machinery was not piled up or even crowded together. A person could meander through this maze without difficulty. The trail to the pasture was a zigzag path around this old rusty stuff.

Ambrose had bought a spring colt (a horse born that spring and recently weaned from its mother). This little guy, Prince, got the benefit of nearly three years of education before he was ridden. The first lesson was that he only had friends at his new home. Much later he learned to run beside Ambrose, who led him with a loose string on his halter. Still later, he was acquainted with a saddle, then a hackamore. All this, and still only the loose string. Ambrose, or Ambe to his cowboy friends, could have buckled on his spurs and ridden any animal that he had a mind to. But this horse would not be bucked out. Gentle had been the method so far, and he saw no reason to change.

It was in the autumn of one of the years of Prince's education that Ambrose and Margaret left the two-storey farm house to the wind and dust. It was just too big, old and drafty to spend another winter in it. It took countless loads of coal to keep warm during the cold months. They took the kids and furniture and moved to town. Ambe commuted the eight miles to the farm. On a beautiful June morning, as Ambrose climbed into his Dodge truck to drive to the farm, he said to himself, "It's time to ride down to check the cattle. I have been riding Prince around the corral for a month and it's about time he learned some cow work. I'll ride him today."

In the corral, Jenny, the bay saddle mare with black legs muzzled a Hello to Ambe. After a handshake-type scratch on Jenny's neck, he slipped the bossile style hackamore onto Prince. A bit would not be used on this horse for a while. He was to have a sensitive mouth and handle like power steering in a truck.

Leading the horse to the barn door, the reins were dropped and Prince stood ground-tied. The saddle was old stuff to the pony. Ambe mounted and reined to the left around the machinery to start on the trail to the pasture. At the first Massey Model 27 combine, there was a misunderstanding. Ambe wanted to go on the left side, whereas Prince chose the right side. Prince won.

"When we came to the I.H.C. 21 swather, I was sitting loose in the saddle, very relaxed. The power shaft of the swather was in the old grass. Prince stepped on it and he exploded. The first jump, and I lost both stirrups. As we dodged and bucked through the old junkyard, I could not get back in the saddle properly. I couldn't find a comfortable place to get off amongst the iron so I rode my darndest. That was no tempest in a tea pot. It was a hurricane amongst the old machinery. Most of the time my boots were up at the pommel of the saddle. When we got out in the open, the darn fool still kept bucking. When he was coming up I was going down. He was too dumb to get me off, and I was so smart that I could not fall off. Boy! Oh Boy! I sure took a beating. We went on to the pasture and Prince worked fine after he had used up that spurt of energy.

Back in town, I had problems getting away from the dinner table. Margaret told me to go and lie on the bed for a while. I did that for three days. I was still stiff and sore, but life got kind of dull, so I got dressed and drove to the hotel. I parked as close to the door as I could and hobbled in. All my buddies whooped and hollered because I was crippled up. That was before mixed drinking. There were no women in the bar room.

I undone my belt and let my blue jeans drop to my ankles. I lifted my shirt and stood there with white jockey shorts. I had one black and blue bruise from my wish bone to my feet. I gave those guys a gunfighter stare and said, "Watch out! You're looking at the Purple Rider of the Sage!"

Beaver

Primeau's farm was on the edge of the forest. Their house was not a mansion, never the less it was adequate, clean and comfortable. Mrs. Primeau's prize possession was the large table in the kitchen. It was made from six different kinds of wood. To build this piece of furniture, her father had made a hand powered lathe to manufacture the legs. The legs were not massive, but turned and carved with love and patience. They were sturdy and graceful. The whole table was beautifully crafted.

Wilfred Primeau's prized possession was the high-powered rifle hanging on the wall. Sure it had a few scratches on the stock, and some of the blue was worn off the metal, but it was extremely accurate. That was why he was proud of it.

One day in the early spring, Mr. Primeau and the game warden were out checking the beaver population along the creek. At one house they heard a whimpering murmur.

"Now that doesn't sound right to me," Wilfred said.

The warden agreed, "Let's open it up and see what gives." When the men cut a hole in the top of the beaver house, the truth was evident. The adult beavers were dead or gone. Six little brown fur balls were doing the whimpering.

"They're out of food, and we've opened the house so now they'll freeze."

"Would your wife look after these guys until they would be big enough to move to where there are no beavers?"

"Let's take them home and ask her."

Mrs. Primeau's heart would go out to any needy creature. Her answer to that question was, "Let's take a few boards and build a little pen in the corner beside the stove."

While Mr. Primeau and the warden were building the walls for the beaver pen, Mrs. Primeau gave each little animal a bit of protein fortified milk with an eye dropper. It was not too many days until the little fellows had graduated from milk to willow bark. Their foster mother would cut a bundle of willow shoots, each about two feet long.

The sticks were propped up in the corner of the pen. Each beaver would get a stick in its front paws, sit on its hind legs and balance with its flat tail, and enjoy the meal. When the eating was finished, Mrs. Primeau would put a basin with a few inches of water in the pen for the pets to bath themselves. If a beaver was startled when in the basin, it would slap the water with its tail and try to dive. Getting its face to the bottom of the pan, it would resurface with a rather silly look about facing reality. Even though they lived in a human's house, they were still creatures of the forest. The foster family could not take from them the inborn need to recognize danger, as well as the need to chew wood to keep their teeth from growing too long. What intriguing house pets! Not only hours, but weeks were spent watching the little bodies grow as well as their antics. The beavers in the pen were a never-ending source of interest.

Mr. Primeau worked hard in the fresh air. He needed rest, and usually slept very soundly. About 2:00 a.m., he was gently nudged by his wife.

"Wilfred, there is something wrong in the kitchen. I heard a thump."

"It is nothing. Go back to sleep."

At 2:30 a.m. "Wilfred, I heard another thump."

"It's nothing."

Much later, "Wilfred there was another thump in the kitchen."

"Don't let your imagination run wild. Let's get some sleep."

At the first light of dawn, the Primeaus arose as usual. What was not usual were the chairs. Each was laying at a crazy angle. One leg had been chewed off every chair. There at the table was the largest of the beaver family, sitting on his hind legs and tail. He had worked all night on the table leg and had it within two bites of being off.

In relating the incident, Mrs. Primeau finished with, "By ten o'clock that morning, it was goodbye to the beavers. The little devils were flying north, on a one way ticket."

Bad Brakes

The outside air was crisp and cool on that particular evening. In Palmer's living-room the thermostat was set for solid comfort. Our wives were in the kitchen making sandwiches and coffee. Pete and I were utterly relaxed, each in an arm chair. The potted jade tree, wood grain panelling and soft light all added to the feeling of comfort.

"It surely is a beautiful night," ventured Pete.

I was in complete agreement. "I had a tune-up and brake job on the Chevy today. We should have a good trip home." It must have been my remark of the good trip home, or the cold full moon that stirred Pete's memory:

"It was just after Waldeck changed from a cattle shipping point to a farming community. In earlier times, thousands of cattle were shipped here by rail from Texas and South Dakota. The stock would be trailed south to the Turkey Track ranch, or north across the river to the Matador ranch. After the fall round up, this was a busy town. Train loads of cattle were shipped to Chicago or Winnipeg, some even going as far as Great Britain."

Pete explained, "Prices were very unstable, up and down, but mostly down at the whim of the elevator companies. The local farmers decided to have a meeting here in town to find ideas that would help the farm economy. There were two farmers up on the rise, across the flat. The nearest was Mr. Jovial, a big man, successful, friendly, and not inclined to worry. On the next quarter section was a neighbour the direct opposite, in every way - a Mr. Timid Soul. On the evening of the meeting, Mr. Jovial hitched up his snappy black buggy team. He generously went to give his neighbour a ride to town. It took a lot of persuasion to get Mr. Timid to go along. He had not had enough time to figure the pros and cons of going to a meeting on a cool, moonlit October night.

Buggies of that era were of two basic designs. There was the end spring model which had a spring mounted on each axle. The center of the upper half of the front spring was attached to the front of the floor or body. The rear spring was attached to the rear end of the buggy floor. This arrangement made for a back and forth action to dissolve the bumps.

The other model was the side spring buggy. This one had larger, longer springs, that were mounted on each side. This system was supposed to give the ultimate smooth ride. One side or the other could absorb a bump. Mr. Jovial's buggy was the side spring model. On the trip to town Mr. Timid did not weigh enough to level out the spring on his side of the buggy, but that didn't matter. He had to hold on to the curved ornamental seat bracket so he would not slide onto Mr. Jovial's lap. The team quickly trotted the few miles into town.

The feeling was the same all over western Canada. There had to be a better way of marketing grain. The glory that these quarter section farmers had imagined being theirs when they homesteaded, was being badly tarnished by scandalously poor grain prices. After enough cigar and pipe smoke had clouded the hall, the meeting was adjourned. This gathering had not produced any syndicate shattering resolutions.

"Well, it's still early, let's have a drink," suggested Mr. Jovial, as he stopped his team at the hitch rack in front of the hotel.

"You go ahead if you wish, I'll stay with the rig," said Mr. Timid, as he tried to wrap his denim smock around his slight frame. As time passed he would wrap it tighter to offset the night chill.

When Jovial did finally come from the bar room he was in a happy frame of mind. He loudly proclaimed, "You should have come in Timid. Most of the boys were there. They are a great bunch of guys."

"The team is getting restless. We better go home," was Timid Souls only thought. They crossed the creek, and now the horses were moving at a right smart trot. Jovial tried to sing, but it didn't sound as good as it did in the hotel. Then he was going to tell the joke that he heard in the bar room, but decided not to. It might be beyond the bachelor's comprehension, and it might be too raw for the little guy. He laughed out loud just thinking about it.

The horses had increased the pace considerably.

"Ar... are... aren't we going too fast?" questioned Timid, with a stutter.

"Nothing to worry about," Jove said with all the confidence in the world. He expertly flipped the left driving line over the off horse, where it dragged in the dirt beside the buggy wheel. In a quick motion the other line was dragging by the right wheel. Without control of a driver, the horses were on their way home in a big rush. Hooves were really drumming on the hard road.

"I can stop them any time you say the word," Jovial said to his companion, who was hanging on for dear life.

Timid Soul finally found enough voice to say "S... S... Stop!"

Mr. Jovial's plan was to grab the right rear wheel and hold it from turning until the horses got tired and stopped. Although the plan was imperfect, Jove tried it anyway. With his gloved hand he made a lightning grab for the back wheel. By clutching the face of the wheel his arm was jerked far down which also compressed the spring on Jove's side. It was pulled right down. By losing his grip on the wheel, his side of the buggy snapped right up to normal. Jovial, off balance, was flung in an arc to land prone at the side of the road.

Now Mr. Timid was alone in the buggy. If he had the nerve he would have jumped, if he had wings he would have flown away. He had neither, so he just sat there. The beauty of the countryside, flooded with moonlight, was lost on Mr. Timid. The breakneck speed of the black horses terrified the lone passenger of the buggy. At one point he opened his mouth to scream, but the wind ballooned his cheeks and forced the sound back to where it came from. To complete the trip, Timid sat as a horrified statue. The team ended their runaway at Jove's closed barn door.

Mr. Timid Soul shakily got out, gathered up the driving lines, and brave beyond belief, drove back to rescue Jove. Jovial, had regained his breath and walked a few steps toward home. When Timid drove back to near the disaster site, he gladly relinquished the lines to the owner. Then Mr. Timid spoke with authority, "YOU SHOULDN'T HAVE OTTA DONE THAT!"

Compromise

I phoned Shirley to let her know that her car was painted and ready to go.

"We aren't too busy at the store today. I'll be there for it later."

"If there was going to be trouble, I would want to be on the same side as Harry." That was the first I had heard of this Indian. James was a powerful, big guy. Holding a heavy log, he said, "If Harry was looking for trouble, I'd be mighty scarce."

A Cree neighbour said, "My sister's boy Harry, wish him home. He can fix my truck. He lay on ground, hold transmission one hand, put bolts in other hand."

When I did meet Harry, I was impressed! White teeth, brown eyes, clear complexion, and black hair. The muscle that covered his six foot frame would do well on a mountain lion.

John and I moved Shirley's car to the finished row. We put a crunchy half ton in the shop to warm up during coffee break. As we neared the house, Harry rounded the corner of the driveway. He brought Shirley to get her Plymouth.

"Just in time for coffee," I greeted them.

"Thanks, some other time," and Shirley was gone.

"Well, I'll try one. I'm not doing much." With that Harry joined us. At the kitchen table with steaming mugs, John faced me, Harry sat facing the window.

"One time at a dance at the lake, a scrap got going good when the RCMP drove in. After they got it cooled down the police told Harry that he had to come to town. He good naturedly climbed in the Paddy Wagon. At the police station they asked him to empty his pockets. Harry asked why. They said he had to surrender his possessions before they locked him up. He told them, "You guys asked me to come to town but locking up was not in the deal." So Harry and three cops wiped the calendars off the wall, and rearranged the furniture."

John told this as if Harry were miles away.

I turned to Harry and asked, "Is that true?"

59

He smiled and answered, "Not exactly, but I never have been locked up."

I surmise they reached a compromise.

Chuck

The ranch was a beautiful place to live. Open meadows, aspen groves, high timber stands, all blended to make a pretty picture. It did consist of two separate leases. Each was administered by different government departments.

The ground hog, or woodchuck, lived under the oil shed. It was a little old wooden building about eight feet square. Inside was a drum of oil, a pail of grease, funnels, measuring cans, and the things common to the upkeep of trucks and tractors.

That stuff was on the main floor, the woodchuck leased the basement where he made his home. In the four years that we were fellow travellers down the road of life, I never did see him eating. In the winter I did not see him at all. This little brown animal was slightly larger than Ginger, the yellow tom cat, who left home in his later years.

It took the woodchuck some months to get his house in order. After that, he spent a lot of time laying right by the door of the oil shed, in the sun. The shop was just far enough from the shed, that a fire in either one would not be a complete disaster. Rowdy, the small cattle dog, made a game of dashing to the woodchuck's lounge, and scaring the little animal back into his hole. It was a game on the dog's part. He never barked or scratched up the dirt sleeping pad by the oil shed door.

The second year that the woodchuck lived with us, Rowdy became peed off with losing every game. I was replacing a broken standard on the bush disc. The machine was in front of the shop. The dog went into a stealthy crouch and sneaked around the building, passed the lumber pile and corral rails, Then, he was coming along the trees to the oil shed. At the right moment he dashed out, grabbed the woodchuck by the back of the neck and raced up to me. He dropped the animal right at my feet.

The woodchuck got his long sharp teeth going so fast that the sound was more like an industrial machine. He was about three feet from me, with his teeth just a buzzing. He made a horizontal motion, threatening my left leg, then threatened my other shin. Turning to the dog, he made a motion as though sawing a vertical slice. With that he gave us a cool look, and turned toward his diggings. He did not rush, but walked with insulted dignity. I said to Rowdy, "The little son-of-a-gun sure has nerve to burn. He warned us that he would cut my legs off, and with you it would be your head." Rowdy gave up the game. He had won once, but never played it again. When I was refuelling a tractor at the shed, (it was right beside the storage tanks) the wood chuck would only retreat far enough so he could watch me.

"You know Chuck, you are a clever looking animal." This was the start of many conversations. The Versatile tractor took a long time to fill the fuel tanks.

"Chuck, how can I get the government to change the lease from grain to grazing? Some bureaucrat made a mistake, and the whole darn department is backing that decision. You know, if the government employees had to do piece work, and get paid for what they did, it would be better. If they made a mistake they would not have to be hung, if they were smart enough to correct it." I thought Chuck agreed with me.

Another day I put the diesel hose to the tractor tank and opened the valve. "You know Chuck this place is half rated for grain, and the rest for grass. I think it would make good hay land." Chuck seemed to nod his head in agreement. The fuel tank was full so I had to go.

The combine had to be driven past the oil shed, then backed in to reach the gas hose. That day Chuck came out farther. "What do you know about that? I harvested eighteen acres and put the whole darn crop in a five-gallon pail. All of this ground is so low and wet that you can't get it seeded in time to beat the fall frost. The government says it is good for barley. At three pounds per acre, that would bring me darn near a dollar income off of that field. It just doesn't pay. It would grow hay like a son of a gun, then I could keep more cows, but try to tell them that, it's hopeless."

"The lease fees have tripled on the grain land, and the barley still freezes." Again Chuck saw it my way.

The next summer I hooked up to the baler, and had it running very slow while I drove a few hundred yards around the row of trees by the oil shed, and stopped at the first hay swath. I got off the tractor to let the baler pickup down to working position. Here Chuck jumped out of the feeder chamber of the baler, where he had been snoozing. That surprised me, and so did the fact that Chuck, with a bamboozled walk, went straight home.

The next summer Glen and Karen were home. They were going to the lake for the weekend. Glen had gassed up his car at the fuel tank, and brought it to the driveway by the house. Rowdy just went nuts with barking at the left front fender of the white Ford. When I was called, there, under the hood and beside the engine, sat Chuck. He would not move. I felt that on the way to the lake he may fall down and get hurt, so I took the garden hose and sprayed cold water on him. That did it! He got down but instead of going northwest to his place, he went southwest, past the barn, through the corrals, into the calving pasture and just kept going. He just walked away.

My soul mate had taken a job in town to support me, while I tried to support the cows. The next year I felt abused like Chuck, so I just walked away too.

63

Looking Back

The prairie land had all been allotted to the homesteaders. There was a dwelling on nearly every half section of farmable soil. There were lots of people but there were also shortfalls. Doctors and hospitals were often far away. Roads to medical help were long, rough and sometimes impassable. Each community had one person or another that was called on in time of emergency. Their skills varied, some were helpful, some were a comfort and still others were great.

Aunt Emma Newton had all these skills and more. She had no formal medical training, but as a young housewife her knack was developed by doctoring horses, cattle, sheep and finally people. One evening, Snap, the young black saddle horse, had his own little stampede. He ran between some machinery and sliced the skin on his side. This foot-long gash was shaped like a stretched button hole. Aunt Emma mixed a three-ingredient recipe, pine tar, acid, and something else. This was boiled in a pan on the stove. When it cooled, the top portion was poured out and the remainder painted on the cut on Snaps' belly. A few applications of this, and the edges of the wound were drawn together and healed over.

I phoned Eleanor Button to see if she remembered the recipe that her mother used in the horse wound stuff.

"No all I remember is that I cried a lot because I was sure I was going to lose my horse," was her answer.

There was that winter day that Aunt Emma went to Ramsden's Store at Hallonquist to buy a supply of groceries. Just when she opened the door, she heard Mrs. Ramsden scream for Mary. Sixteen-year-old Mary was working in the storeroom and at the call, she rushed out to see blood pouring down her mother's leg. The lady had been using the back edge of the hatchet to split a large lump of coal that was too big to fit in the stove. The tool glanced off the coal and put a bad cut in Mrs. Ramsden's leg.

Neither Aunt Emma nor Mary stopped to ask what happened. They got the injured one sitting in a nearby chair.

"Mary, get two pounds of tea." With that Aunt turned to the dry goods counter and slashed off a yard of white cotton cloth. With Mrs. Ramsden's foot resting on another chair, Mary held the cloth by its ends, making a sling for the injured leg. Aunt poured the tea leaves on the wound. With two pounds of tea on the sore spot, the bleeding slowed down. Carefully, the yard of cotton was wrapped around the bleeding leg, bandaging the wound and the tea in one large bulge. In a very short time the blood had stopped oozing out.

"There you go, Mrs. Ramsden. Get plenty of rest and eat liver and green vegetables, if you can get them this time of year."

That was the completion of successful first aid. Mary gave Aunt Emma full credit for saving her mother's life.

Another case happened right at home that summer. Aunt had become thoroughly disgusted with Steve, one of the hired men.

"Ben, why don't you fire that guy? I'm sick and tired of him coming every Monday morning, wanting something for his hangover. He has drunk up every bit of fruit salts that I had."

"Now Mother, he is a real good man, a good worker and trustworthy. We will have to put up with his weekend sprees."

Monday morning came and so did Steve. At the back door of the kitchen he asked, "Would you have something to help clear my head? I sure feel tough this morning."

Aunt Emma told us later that on that morning, she was in the midst of making a batch of pickles. In wholesome disgust she filled a large tumbler with red pickling vinegar. Now, that was strong stuff. Even a little bit of it made the pickles kind of sharp. Steve was sitting on the back step holding his aching head with his hands.

"Here Steve, get this down. You will soon feel different."

In a few minutes Steve came in, handed over the empty tumbler and said, "Say, Mrs. Newton, you must have been quite a rounder in your day. That sure straightened me up."

If she had ever been nominated for the Nobel Prize for medicine, she would have considered the curing of Steve as the reason for the award.

They Tried Harder

I was not having a good day. One difficulty after another had made me somewhat grouchy. Maybe grouchy is not the right word, but it was a time that a smile would not be uppermost. It seemed that the harder I tried, the more difficult my work became. Then, a break from the rolled-over truck job! The shop foreman called me to a small problem with the vehicle parked behind my stall. The car was a two-tone green Buick Roadmaster, a two-door hardtop with nylon upholstery. The light green seats were patterned with embroidered dark green fleurs-de-lis. This was a car you did not jump into. You would slide in behind the wheel, to glide away with power and luxury.

The work order read, "Recall Hood Lock Kit and Adjustment." This meant that I was to go to the Parts Dept. and get a special reinforcing plate, then open the hood and, from the underside, remove the lock nut, place the little square plate on the lock pin, replace the nut, adjust the hood lock, and tighten the lock nut again.

The owner of this fine auto had been a senior citizen for some years. He was standing watching me.

"They don't make them like they used to." His little speech grated on my nerve. I thought that just because his hood would pop up and ride on the safety catch every time that he hit a bump, he was condemning the whole car.

He repeated, "They don't make them like they used to." Just then my wrench slipped, my knuckles got thumped.

Under my breath I muttered, "If the old goat says that one more time I'll feel like slugging him." You see I was still having a bad day.

"They don't make them like they used to, thank goodness." The 'thank goodness' was what made me stop to listen:

"It was in 1914 that I got a 1912 Franklin Touring Car. It had an air cooled-motor, and the frame was made of Ash Wood. All the metal parts were cold rivetted to the frame, like the spring hangers and body mount arms." He continued, "Them days we always dressed up on

67

Sundays. With a good suit, a white shirt, a celluloid collar, a neck tie, and with a hat, you were dressed up. You always had your shoes shined."

"On a sunny Sunday afternoon in November, it was warm as summer. There were six of us that got in my car to go for a drive. We had two cases of Sicks Lethbridge Pilsner beer with us. In them days, when you got a case of beer, there were twenty-four in a box. Each one had its own gray paper coat. That's what kept them from jingling. I suppose it kept the sun off and helped to keep em cool."

"In them days there was no bridge across the river here. We drove south to the old Fort Whoop Up. There we crossed the Old Man River on the sand bars. We angled northwest and drove on prairie grass that was dry cured and still a foot high. Out between Monarch and Kipp there was enough winter grazing for hundreds of cattle. It was out there that my fuel line leaked. The wind whipped the gas over to the frame. The exhaust was hot enough to ignite the gas on the wooden frame. There we were, eight miles from the river, and that was the nearest water. We had just finished the last beer, and my car was on fire. The only thing we could do, was raise the hood, and take turns standing with one foot on the engine the other on the fender. We unbuttoned and squirted at the fire." Tapping my chest with his fore finger, "You would be surprised how fast your turn would come after the second round!" With a mild grin he added, "Yes sir, we saved my car."

To Gain Experience

Norman and I were replacing the windshield in John Sr.'s car. He informed us that human life is not unending.

That is how the Norwegian born, building contractor of St. Paul, Minnesota passed on. His millions were to be disposed of according to his will. This document was well planed. No benefactor could find fault with it. The fact that he bequeathed a large sum to a certain Seminary in southern Minnesota, and the condition attached to the gift proved his mental competence. The money had to go for the purchase of a pipe organ. The size of the instrument was spelled out exactly. It was huge. The price was calculated and increased by sixty percent, just as a precaution. The whole deal required that an addition had to be built onto the chapel, to house the monster. The addition contained only the pipes for the organ, and a clothes rack along the outer wall. During the hot humid summer this was a forgotten area.

On Tuesday, 2:37 P.M., there was a loud bang from this location, a very, very loud bang. The noise brought the senior clergymen on the run. There they saw the damage and debris! A large dent in each of the two biggest organ pipes, seven damaged choir gowns, some damage to the wall, and assorted parts of a homebrew still. At 2:41 P.M. the official inquiry had begun. The students responsible were soon found out. After all they were to be clergymen of the future - truth was part of their life. They admitted to building and operating the still. With all the evidence lying around, even a hardened criminal would've confessed.

July 2,
Dear Sir,

Your son, a student at our Seminary was found guilty of distilling alcohol on college property. Besides the sin committed, a great deal of damage was done. He will be expelled immediately.

Yours Truly,
Dean...

69

When these nine letters crossed the State line to Iowa, there certainly was a reaction. Nine mothers were distraught. Nine fathers formed an action group.

"Swenson, you write down what we think and be our secretary."

Iowa
July 5,
Dear Dean,

Send us an estimate of the damage. We will pay it. Do not expel the boys until we have more talks.

Yours Truly,
Swen...

A corn fog settled over Iowa. Righteous indignation settled over the college.

Minn.
July 7,

The costs are as follows:
Wall...
Pipes...
Gowns...

Yours Truly,
Dean...

"Ya, da vall and da gowns I can see. Da pipes is too damn much."

"Vell Ole, I tink we got to go with dem prices. Our boys are in trouble."

Minn.
July 10,

Received your cheque, thank you. The sacrilegious act of your sons cannot go unheeded.

Yours Truly,
Dean...

The seminary feathers were still ruffled.

Iowa
July 12,

How much of your annual budget comes from our five congregations? What would the result be if this support was lost?

Yours Truly,

Swen...

The corn and beans were growing like crazy.

Minn.
July 13,

Your donations amount to 28 percent of our annual income. To not have your help and goodwill would be devastating.

Yours Truly,

Dean...

Iowa
July 15,

Making home brew in church isn't a thing to be proud of, but how much better for a Minister to lead if he has walked the path rather than read it in a book.

Yours Truly,

Swen...

Minn.
July 17,

The boys are doing very well. It is commendable the way they study.

Yours Truly,

Dean...

John Sr. ended, "So help me, that's true. Them Scandinavians blackmailed the seminary and got away with it."

A Cup Full

Victrina Gaumond put the tea and cookies on the table and seated herself. What better time to visit the neighbours than on a chilly winter night. The four of us, John, Victrina, Berniece and myself were sipping tea around the kitchen table. It was only natural that we would talk about the old times.

Victrina remembered, "My Great-Grandmother was married when she was seventeen. It was in the autumn, at St. Bonaface. They were married in the morning and had to run from the church to get on the boat. Her man worked on a supply boat. The boat took stuff to the fur trading posts and mine camps up north among the lakes and rivers.

They decided to get married and spend their honeymoon on the last trip of the season. They did not call it a honeymoon. I don't think that they had honeymoons at St. Bonaface in them days. If the parents could afford it, they would celebrate after the church wedding by eating and dancing. Most of the time it was a matter of work so you could eat the next day.

If she would not have married him, she may have married someone that would have taken her west, onto Wood Mountain or Willow Bunch with the Red river cart brigade, to make pemican.

They sailed north for many days. Sometimes they had to stop because of storms. When they got to the last camp and unloaded supplies, the weather turned so cold that some of the narrows froze over and they would not get home. So they stayed at the camp until spring.

Great-Grandmother was a pretty Indian girl and the only woman in the whole camp. The miners treated her with great respect. Her husband worked on the boat in the day time, and there was nothing for a seventeen-year-old girl to do. She borrowed a big kettle, a tub and wash board from the trading post. She carried water from the lake and heated it in the big kettle. That was a lot of work, chopping a hole in the ice to get water, then carry the water to fill the iron kettle, then chop wood for a fire to boil the wash water, then carry hot water into the cabin to the tub, then rub the dirty clothes on the scrub board until the clothes were clean, then twist as much water out of them as she could, then take the clothes out and hang them across the rope tied between two trees, then after they were frozen, she would shake as much frost off as she could and take them in the cabin and hang them up to dry.

When she got their clothes all washed, she did some for the miners. Then she spent the rest of the winter washing clothes for the men of the camp. She did this like a hobby for something to do. The men gave her a grain of gold once in a while. Some gold was like a flax seed. Some was like a green pea. She sewed a leather bag to put the gold in.

By spring the bag had enough gold to fill a tea cup. When they got to Winnipeg, a man offered her five dollars for the bag of gold. She had no use for it, so she sold it."

"How much would that be worth today?" Mrs.Gaumond asked. No one present had even seen gold nuggets. There followed some wild estimates as to the weight of gold to fill a tea cup. "The price of gold last week was $382 an ounce." That was the only definite fact we had to go on. The value of a cup full of gold was still a hazy guess.

Victrina summed it up, "Things and time and people change. But it would be nice to have Great-Grandma's $5 bag of gold."

That Must Have Hurt

When we were kids, Albert was a stocky, muscular, square jawed, young fellow. His deep voice so easily gave out that catchy laugh. With a devil-may-care personality in that strong body, Albert was usually followed by adversity. He generally wrestled it right to the ground and came out on top. In short, he was pioneer tough. It must still be that way for him. As a senior citizen, he is a member of the Prairie Greyhound Association.

Albert went to the United States to acquire better stock to improve his pack of racing dogs. After very careful selecting, he returned with two greyhounds. The male dog had such an impressive race record! On the oval track, he made the electric rabbit use just about every last one of his volts.

The female was a younger animal. Her genetic background was fast, fast, fast. This pair of super dogs had cost a multitude of dollars. Just to prove the great speed of the animals, at the last race of the season, Albert entered his new father-type greyhound. The Prairie People run their dogs in a straight path, no oval track or mechanical bunny for these guys. Their racers go for the tail of an executed renegade coyote. It travels a quick one hundred yards on a cable. Out of the gate like a shot, Albert's dog angled to the left like he had been accustomed to. He missed the rabbit, so he took mighty leaps in the air to help spot the varmint.

The crowd of spectators had no chance to get out of the way of this dog that had lost his property. He considered the rabbit his very own. With mighty leaps and bounds he made his way through the spectators, and on across the stubble field. When last seen he was still moving east at a sensational speed.

All was not lost. Albert still had the female. Somewhere he would find a suitable mate for her. Even the first litter of pups could make the investment a profitable one.

Our friend lives alone on the farm quite remote from neighbours. One day he was milling feed, into the old wooden granary.

On the last few seconds of the job the mill started to plug. The drive belt was loose and slipping. To get over the last little lump and get the thing finished, Albert grabbed a stick and slapped between the belt and pulley. Accidents will happen. Albert's arm also went between the belt and pulley, but only half way around. That much arm, wedged in so small a space, stalled the motor but it left him on his knees, with his right arm half twisted out of its shoulder socket.

Being all alone on such a cold day, only his own cool nerve could save his life. He walked his feet up the side of the wooden building so he could hang by his toes from a board under the eves. That move relieved some of the pressure that was threatening to dislocate his shoulder. With his left hand he got his jackknife from his right jean pocket, opened the blade and cut the belt to free himself.

Someone asked, "That must have really hurt?"

"No," he replied, "while I was cutting the belt, to get loose from the feed mill, my old collie was breeding the greyhound. THAT REALLY HURT!"

One Tree

Larry and his older brother, Leonard, had logged in the winter. They sawed and planed the lumber in the spring and summer. Now, it was early autumn and time for harvest. "Say Leonard, how would it be if we take a load of lumber down south? The farmers will be building granaries. They need the boards and we could use the money," was Larry's inspiration.

"Sure, I'll load it and you take it. It's your idea."

At North Battleford, Larry learned the awful truth. The south country was dried out. They had no crops at all. A wasted day and the night that followed proved that Larry had a problem. There was no sale for lumber. No use trucking it home again. There were piles of the stuff at home as it was. About the time the problem was approaching dilemma status, a farmer came along.

"I see you have a For Sale sign on your lumber. How much you asking?"

With his most friendly smile, Larry said, "Well, this is your lucky day. I'm in a good mood and the price is dirt cheap."

After a long, long visit and friendly negotiations it seemed dirt cheap was still beyond the budget of this guy. The wood buyer finally made the winning offer.

"If you will bring it out to the farm, I will trade you a Ford half ton for your lumber. You can get home and start harvesting. I'll get the boards off of your truck, and bring it as far as Glaslyn next week." Then he added, "I'm plenty used to International R models, we've had one for years."

After a hearty dinner at the farm house, Larry started home in his new eight-year-old Ford half ton truck. It was not a great deal, just a good deal. No cash, but still a good deal. Yes, a good deal until he came to the long downhill grade on number three highway. He was rambling right along gaining speed by the minute. There, down the road a ways, were two vehicles parked side by side. Of all things! Two neighbours visiting in the middle of the road. When he neared the parked trucks, Larry touched his brake pedal but nothing happened. Larry jumped on his brake pedal. Nothing happened. Seeing that he could not stop, he took to the ditch. That seemed to be the only choice - no options.

He rolled the truck, a complete upset. The fellows that were the reason for the misfortune did help Larry get his Ford back on its wheels. He went on his way with a much crunched truck with no windows and no windshield. In fact he was short most of the things every other truck had. The rest of the trip was uneventful, breezy, but uneventful.

The driveway to the farmyard was narrow and winding. As Larry made the half way point, he heard Leonard coming out with the one ton truck that had the broken exhaust and it sounded loud. Knowing that he would meet Leonard at the next curve, Larry chose a fair-sized aspen tree to stop against. The top of the tree snapped off and came to rest on the roof of the new eight-year-old Ford half ton. At least he was out of Leonards way. His big brother came to a stop, and looked at Larry's truck. The hood, fenders, doors, roof, box and anything else that could dent was dented.

"How could one tree make such a mess?" Leonard asked.

Mapping the Backwoods

"It was just one of those days that makes you want to live forever. Blue sky, yellow aspens and green spruce. It was warm with a soft breeze. A perfect fall day, until I had the darn flat tire about seven miles south of Big River," was the opening of Charlie's description of the episode.

In earlier years, Charles lived at Leoville, then he got a farm at Big River. There, he bought building moving equipment as well. He travelled a long way to get the trucks, beams, dollies and jacks.

His plan was to get the stuff home, move a couple of shacks for experience and get into business. On the way home he was beseeched, implored, begged and pleaded with, to move homes seven different times. "My goodness! By the time we got home we had a pile of experience. We went right to work."

During the ensuing years, Charlie has been in most every district from Saskatoon north, and border to border. And he never forgets a name. On this particular day, friend Charlie had finished changing the flat tire, when a car with six ladies stopped to ask directions.

"Mister, could you please tell us how to get to Spiritwood?" asked the person in the front passengers seat.

"But of course," Charles replied, "Just turn around and go back to Shellbrook, then turn right on number three highway."

"Do you know how we could get from Spiritwood to Leoville?"

"But, to get to Leoville, you don't have to go back to number three highway. You go back nine miles and turn right."

"Just a moment," interrupted one lady as she extracted a writing pad from her purse, "Let us get the direction right on paper."

"All right, turn around and go south until you go by the store. You can't miss it. There are gas pumps out in front. The store will be on your left. A bit farther on, there will be cat tails growing on your right. When you get to the top of the hill just past the cat tails, turn right on the gravel road. Where you cross the railway track, there is a tricky little curve, go cautiously there... Green farm house, turn right... big spruce bluff, turn left.... past lake, ...turn right at brown and white house,.... follow main road, ...there will be a T intersection turn right. That will get you to number 24 highway. There, make a right, turn and two miles on you will be in Leoville." With all this on the homemade map with descriptive land marks, no one could get lost. "Do you know how to get to Chitek Lake from Leoville?"

"But of course I do. To get to Chitek Lake, you turn left just at the edge of Leoville." Then Charlie asked "Who would you be looking for at the lake?"

"We are school teachers from Regina. We are going to see Mrs. Riel, the principal of the Chitek Lake Indian School."

"Oh, but ladies you don't go to the lake to find Helen. When you go past the Penn store one and a half miles, you turn left. Go west six miles. There will be an intersection, with the hall on your right, the school and church on your left. Across the road from the church there is a farm yard with steel granaries. That is where Mrs. Riel lives."

"How far is it to where Mrs. Riel lives?"

At that, Charlie had to look around at the spruce tops to get his bearings. "It is seventy-eight miles."

"How would you know Mrs Riel, if she lives that far away?"

Charlie got a nearly hurt look on his face, "Ladies, this is a big country and we have to depend on our neighbours."

For a Cup of Tea

Minutes after my wife had finished helping me with chores, I turned on the pipe-line and milker washer, set the switches and went to the house. Our day had begun fifteen hours earlier, like every other day for the last six years. Sleep would be most welcome, even sympathy would be appreciated.

The transition from grain farming to dairying had not been so hard, but the welfare of sixty cows, and forty of those had to be milked twice a day, required more work and time than we had ever imagined. Mother was visiting with us and I had promised to drive her home to Herbert after milking. After an exchange of countless topics with her grandchildren, and a lengthy farewell, she got into the Chev. Approaching the main road I asked, "Would you care to see the land that I had a chance to buy last spring?"

"Well if it's not too far out of the way, it would be all right," she replied.

"It's along the north road. It will be about fifteen miles more but there is still an hour of daylight." A few miles farther on the way, I waved a hand to the right and pointed out the slough, the hills, the rocks and grass. It was a thing of the past and did not require slowing down to see.

We travelled north to the correction line, then east nine miles and a right turn to the south. There, Mom became very alert. Until then the drive had been without conversation, we were just enjoying the summer evening.

"Look at that farm over on the right side of the road! My how those trees have grown. We thrashed there in 1914. My cousin and I ran the cook car. She was eighteen and I was sixteen. We cooked for about thirty men."

I mentally calculated that the trees had been growing there for sixty-one years. In that time they would be somewhat larger, but I kept quiet.

Mother continued, "We had moved late in the afternoon, and that always slowed us down. We couldn't work or rest while our cook car was hauled down the road. It was rough and bouncy. The road was not graded then, just a prairie trail. That meant we had to work faster to get the meal on for the thrashing crew.

The last of the men were just seated at the table when the farmer came to the door. He asked us to come to their house for a cup of tea. We turned down the invitation because we would have to work until near midnight to have things in shape for the next day. Then, he begged us to come. He claimed that his wife had no feminine company since she had arrived from England. We still had too much work to do to go out for tea. Then he asked us to please come, because she was so lonesome.

One of the men said that we should go on over, that there was enough food on the table and they would be all right. So we took off our aprons and went across the yard to their house. Sure enough, this English lady made tea and served it in fine china cups. She did seem to appreciate our being there. We gulped our tea and were ready to go. She refilled our cups, and talked a blue streak. Then her husband came in, more tea and he took over the talking.

We could not relax and enjoy the tea party. There were all of the dishes to wash, and a small mountain of pots and pans to scrub. There were the potatoes to peel and vegetables to clean. Oh! It seemed that we had a million things that would have to be done before we could go to bed. The man would glance out the window every once in a while.

One time, the window in the cook car was dark. So, the last one at the table blew out the lamp. I thought that was just as well as to leave it burning with no one there. It seemed to me that we had been held prisoner for hours. It was only nine o'clock when he moved the window drape again. There I saw our lamp shining brightly in our window. Well, that was it, we had to go!

We thanked our hostess and hurried back to work. When we stepped in our door, flabbergasted would not describe our feelings. The floor was swept. The table and benches had been washed. All of the dishes were washed and set back on the table ready for breakfast. We used to put the cups and plates on upside down at each place so they were clean and handy for the next meal. All the kettles were clean and put away. There were potatoes peeled, and covered with water, the carrots were the same way. There was coal, wood and water for the morning. Even one little kettle with a potato simmering on the stove, all ready for starter for the next days bread baking. All that we had to do was get the starter in the potato water, and we were finished for the day. The thrasher crew surely did a put up job on us. While the farm people were soaking us with tea, there must have been half of the men in doing our work. They had hung a coat over the window so we would not know what they were up to. We sure were a pair of grateful girls."

The next time that I felt overworked, all I had to do was think of how those two teenage girls had to work. As for me, there was no dreaming of tea with an English couple.

From the Daily Paper

OSLO Norway(AP)[1]

Norway has very strict laws against drinking and driving. But not as strict as police thought, when they detained and fined a man for driving his electric wheelchair while under the influence[2].

Roar Karlsen left a bar after drinking six beers[3]. In his electric wheelchair, with a top speed of 6.5 km/h, he passed some police officers. He then returned to ask if he was allowed to continue operating his wheelchair since he had been drinking[4]. The police responded by taking Karlsen to the station, testing his alcohol level, and assessing an $850.00 fine[5]. The test showed alcohol in Karlsen's blood of more than three times the legal limit for driving. Police noted he also had a couple more beers with him in the wheelchair[6].

Karlsen refused to pay the fine. A court ruled that, although he was too drunk to drive a car, his wheelchair did not move fast enough to be a hazard[7]. Karlsen told the court his one regret was stopping to talk to the police officers[8].

---

[1] This is a clue that Roar K. is Scandinavian.

[2] Roar is adventurous, and being a Viking, goes exploring.

[3] Grandfather came from Norway, although he did not drink he used to say, "Too much is too much, but too much beer is just right."

[4] That is Norsk. Explore, explore, search out the truth, learn all the facts, know where you stand.

[5] The police must have been on foot when Roar encountered them. With a fine that heavy, they must have been saving up to buy a prowl car.

[6] This expedition could turn into a long dry trip. The extra supplies were good foresight.

[7]That Roar sure slipped that one past the judge. They did not know how much faster the wheelchair was than Lena, the limping lady with a crutch.

[8]Uff Da!

Ski Slope

I was just a little shaver, when I first encountered Scandinavian superstition. On that lazy sunny afternoon, Mother was going to have a cup of tea with Mrs. Benson. A few bits of wood had been put in the kitchen range. The tea kettle was placed at the front of the stove to boil for tea. In the course of time the water did boil. The kettle gave out a homey whistling song. "MOVE THE KETTLE! MOVE THE KETTLE," the hostess fairly shouted. Mother moved the kettle to a cooler spot on the stove top. Mrs. Benson had her hands full. To have tea required, biscuits, preem oust (sour milk cheese), Yeit oust (goat cheese) goose-berry jam and other goodies. When the dear woman got her hands free of food, she folded them and gazed heavenward for a second or two, then she explained, "Every time a kettle sings, a sailor dies at sea."

I had to check this out with Grandpa. He knew everything. The topic of superstition introduced me to a whole regiment of the little make-believe creatures.

This was all in good fun. Grandma's view was, "Pa, don't be so dumb, filling the kid's head with that old stuff. Find something better to talk about." Grandpa and I were having so much fun that we kept on. Our imaginations were running full speed ahead. We could not stop immediately. I do remember the Trolls and that's enough for now.

Sven was in his early twenties, athletic as all get out. As an apprentice, in the building trade, his job was to hew the timbers for the tourist lodge that was being built on the fjord on the coast of Norway. He was a good worker, but he'd rather ski than eat. This guy had so much nerve, people said that he had blue ice in his veins. On May 17, the national holiday, his peers suggested that he ski down from the very top of "Mount Impossible." Sven couldn't disregard a challenge. With full winter dress, skis over his shoulder, his coat pockets full of cheese lumps and speka chet (beef jerky made from mutton), Sven started for the peak of Old Impossible. The mountain was so high that its sharp peak was obscured by clouds for months at a time. Hour after hour of climbing, he did reach the needle-sharp top of the mountain. As Sven looked down at the village, he muttered some cuss words (Holy Cats this is high).

Gomla Trudholm (Captain Eric K. Trudholm, before his retirement) pointed his old seagoing telescope at the tip of Mount Impossible. Through a break in the clouds, the old man saw Sven leave the top of the mountain. Forty feet of skiing and his coat tail was straight out behind. Sven entered the cloud area, (he considered it fog) at a speed much greater than breathtaking. The trolls are invisible, their house invisible too, so the crazy nut, skiing so fast did not see the little people. Sven crashed through the troll's house going about two hundred miles an hour. The Reema Grout, Teata Bere and Flut Bread were scattered all over the place. Not only the dinner, but the entire little house was demolished.

These tiny little Viking-type fairies were just ready to sit down to their meal. Such senseless waste! House, meal, and all, gone in one crash. The matriarch troll was quite upset. "Du Gauv Hake Unddommelig Tomset!" (you fuzzy chinned, young cracked-brain), she scolded. Then she laid on the curse. "He shall be at Lake Athabasca in his underwear." She was old, her nose was long, and she was minus one front tooth. In the rush of anger and the lisp, Athabasca, Canada (which was still ice covered) turned out to be a small resort lake in southern Minnesota, USA

Sven came out of the fog into bright sunlight, skiing on blue water. He was unaware of the Trolls disaster, nor was he aware of the Troll's curse. But this was not the fjord? He was lost, and felt the environmental shock. No, it was a fully developed summer resort.

There on his right was a gorgeous blonde in a blue bikini, skiing behind a jet boat. The sight of this girl certainly neutralized what shock he felt, in fact his metabolism had sped way up. Her beauty would have taken Sven's breath away if he would have had any. He had not had time to breathe since before he crashed the troll's house. To avoid an accident, Sven had to turn left. To a man of his ability this was no problem. But this was water skiing! "Gee, I only knew you could ski on snow," Sven thought.

On his next loop around the lake he was losing momentum. The jet boat finally caught up with Sven, pulling ahead. The blonde lady crossed and recrossed the boat wash. Sven caught on fast. He zig zagged across her tracks. Not daring one more circle of the lake, because he knew that in time, he would lose speed and sink. Heading for the beach was the only thing he could do. The trouble was, he still had too much speed. The Troll's curse and the water skier were disturbing, but Sven was not disturbed, he was confused. Across the sand and over the grass he whizzed. Past the concession booth and into the grove of shade trees with such force the wide heavy mountain skis were totally demolished. Not one sliver of evidence remained. There sat Sven dazed in his boxer shorts. He was just born lucky, (Why he wore such underwear to climb Impossible Mountain is hard to say, but wouldn't he have looked dumb at the beach in long hand knit woolen underwear?)

A crowd soon gathered. One gray-haired gentleman, not a full generation away from the old country said, "By yimmeny, you are yust about as good a skier as my girl Helga. The one you vas skiing vith."

Years passed by, and one day Sven looked out over St. Paul, Minnesota from the office window on the eighteenth floor of his building. "I have Svenson Construction Incorporated. I have my wife Helga, the mother of the skiing Svensons. Now, because of some dumb government forms, some twenty-five-cent bureaucrat from Washington wants to see my birth certificate."

"I think I skied to America, but I just can't explain that to nobody."

Aw, heck when he left home that day, he did not take his birth certificate. He was only going to ski down Old Impossible.

The Red Car

This happened years ago, when muscle cars were the rage. The new models were coming out in September that year. The show room was completely renovated, every little detail that would help to show the new cars at an advantage was taken care of.

The sales manager ordered the vehicle that later got dubbed, "Red Special Order." This car had it all. A huge 348 cubic inch engine, a super torque automatic transmission, all mounted in the brand-new x-tunnelled frame. This was all hidden with the retooled body. There had never been a car so advanced in design available to the motoring public. The trouble was, this wonder car did not arrive in September, but in May the following year.

The extra sales punch of the big engine, heavy tranny, power antenna, dual radio speakers, deluxe trim and countless other unseen features, were lost. All that money tied up in one piece of inventory was enough to have the sales manager tearing out his hair. The only solution was to move the "Red Special Order" fast. Cut the price to the bone, but sell it now.

The next day the red car was the property of an older, discerning gentleman that appreciated fine things and enjoyed life in general. Not many days elapsed until we saw the red car again. This time Charlie brought it back with the tow truck. It was a sorry mess, scratched, dented, shattered glass, really just a twisted piece of junk.

To the assembled service staff, Charlie explained, "The owner lent it to his nephew for his drivers test." As he undid hooks and chains he continued, "You know that husky kid on the football team? Well, he passed the test and got his license, but then he took a dare that he shouldn't have. He bet that he could drive up the motorcycle trail with this car. It was right near the top of the hill that he spun out and had to back down. He did good for the first part, but then he turned to the right into the side hill and rolled to the bottom."

Someone said, "I bet the uncle will be hog wild when he finds out what happened to his car."

Charlie answered, "Na, the old man just dotes on that kid. If he has to, he'll buy a new one to lend him."

"Red Special Order," was pushed into the far corner of the shop and covered with a heavy brown tarpaulin to safeguard any loose parts and to keep away prying eyes.

It was about ten the next morning, when a portly gentleman in a well-tailored suit, and polished shoes entered the shop. With a white handkerchief in his hand, he removed his hat and wiped perspiration from his pink face and balding head. He very politely stated, "I have come to see the damaged red car that was brought in yesterday."

Another snooper I thought, "You can't see it. It has a tarp tied down on it."

"Well, look here! It is my car and I want to see it."

It took some mumbling of words for me to get out an apology. "Come with me." I led him to the red wreck.

He walked with short steps and his toes turned out, a sure sign of his living many years. I untied some of the tarp ropes when the owner stopped me.

"That is good enough. I can see what I want."

I went back to my job, which happened to be repairing the top of a station wagon. A few minutes passed and the man in the gray suit was back.

"I tied up the ropes again, and thank you."

To make up for some of my former rudeness when the customer first came in, I asked, "How is the young fella that was driving your car? Did he get hurt?"

With a mischievous grin the old duffer said, "No. No, I haven't caught him yet." With a chuckle at his own humour he walked away.

We Tried

It must have been in March 1931, because 1932 was too mild and dry a winter to leave deep puddles. One afternoon, on a clear sunny day, I saw Uncle Albert coming to our place. He was using a low box wagon and driving the bay team of Dan and Lady. When he turned off the trail to go around a slough, I could see Aunt Ebba, Basil, Alvin and Scotty, the hired man. Whoopee, Basil was coming! That was good. It was sure great to have someone to do things with. Minutes later they were in the yard. Aunt Ebba and the boys stayed, while the men went to town.

In the house, with the winter wraps off, Basil and I upset the toy box. It was originally a wooden apple box. Now, it held horses, cows, marbles, cars, trucks, tinker toys, dominoes, cap guns, in fact, my whole six years of life savings. While my pal and I were sorting through this pile of treasures on the kitchen floor, the extra leaves were put in the dining room table. A couple of yards of cotton print were laid out and our mothers had a dress under construction.

It was either the distraction factor, or the chance that we would be so noisy and waken Joann, my little sister, or Alvin, my little cousin, who were taking a nap, that we were scooted outside to play.

The barn door was too heavy for us to open, so the barn was free of our investigation. We did climb to the top of the gate at the sheep pen. When the old black-faced ewe with the two new lambs snorted and stamped a foot, I met Basil. He was coming down the inside of the gate, while I was going up and out. The fact that Basil was two years younger than me, sometimes put us out of step. We picked another gate and rested our midriffs on the top plank of that gate and discussed all there was to know about sheep. That finished, we removed a few oat sheaves from the feed stack. That did not prove interesting so we moved on.

Near the telephone pole in the yard, we spotted a steel wheel in the middle of the puddle. This piece of iron had been the land wheel of a horse-drawn plow. It was small enough to roll if we could only get it out. With an exploratory foray into the puddle, I found that I could get my mitts under one edge of the wheel. I also found that the wheel was frozen into ice at the bottom of the mud puddle. I asked for help, but Basil had some reservations. We were supposed to stay clean and dry. More checking, more stomping, more churning and I had our puddle well disturbed.

I learned that there was not much of the wheel in the ice. I gave it a mighty try. My feet slipped. The splash I made had a multiplier effect. The mud and water coming down plastered the part of me that was not sitting in the puddle. I joined my friend on dry ground to better assess the situation.

I searched for a dry bit of coat sleeve to rub across my nose. There was none. I had to use a wet sleeve. It seemed that if we both lifted on the one side it should break free. We each got our mitts under the rim of the wheel and shoulder to shoulder we heaved on the stubborn old plow wheel. Then Basil slipped and went down. He accused me of pushing him. If I did, it must have been because I did not think that he was really working. Or, maybe I had a bad case of industrial stress.

The spring runoff water was getting kind of cold so we gave up and went to the house. Our eyeballs were still fairly clean. Basil got the first bath, and I got a scolding. I got the second bath and the second section of the scolding.

"You are big enough to know better," scrub... scrub... "You should be able to look after your cousin," scrub... scrub... "You should have...."

With dry clothes on we went back and dumped out the toy box.

Blueprint

The blueprint was on a foot long, gray, weather-beaten board. The vertical lines were deep, precise and legible. The horizontal ones across the board, with no wood grain to follow, were not as firm or easy to read. The whole plan being drawn with a bent rusty nail, would make a person think that the drawing and engineering were not architecturally born.

Joe was the owner of the farm, which was located on the edge of the flat plain. The wooded bluffs far northeast of town, started on the corner of this property. In the more prosperous years, before the depression, Sam was the hired man. Now, that status had faded to plain Joe and Sam. The ideal life as these two pictured it, would be a comfortable chair in the hotel beverage room and foamy glasses on the table.

As this was not their station in life, they were building new winter quarters for the pigs. Sam leaned on the last few poles on the wagon. Eyeing the crude framework of the new hog house, he questioned, "Say Joe, shouldn't we put brace poles on each end?"

Joe walked a few steps, and picked up the piece of board that he had scratched the plan on. Waving the scrap of wood he confidently said, "Nope, it just ain't on the blueprint."

Sam was not completely convinced.

Joe directed, "You hitch up the team to the hayrack. We'll go and get some of that rained-on hay that is still in the field. We'll put that on for the roof. While you are getting ready, I'll go and check the mash." Then he added, "I suppose I can start cooking tomorrow morning, if the weather is clear enough for you to be on the lookout for the law."

The mash was fermenting in the secret hole under the porch. The porch was a narrow addition to the house. On the walls hung old winter clothes, one coyote pelt, five weasel skins, and many skunk pelts, all on fur stretchers. There also were a couple of old tin pails containing sour, sloppy kitchen scraps. The purpose of this stinking mess was to hide the odour of the still just beneath the floor.

The afternoon sun had settled behind dark storm clouds. The first snow of the season began to fall when Joe put down his pitch fork.

"Sam, you finish forking the hay on this front corner of the roof. I'll go and check the mash again and get us some supper."

Sam grunted, "Okay." Next he gave a mighty grunt to accompany an extra large fork of hay to its resting place on the aspen pole rafters. The sound began as a snapping branch. As the pig house structure gave way, the sound changed to a crunching crash. The new building rested on the ground in it's own debris.

Sam shook his head and muttered, "Darn lousy blueprint."

Livestock, grain and fur prices were all very low that year. But, all in all, these two old bachelors had a real good winter. The mash was good, the Cop didn't raid the still, and the pigs slept in the straw pile.

Keeping Up

His Buick was the first 1953 model that I had to repair, and he was one of the biggest men I had seen. The mighty men of Stampede Wrestling had nothing on this Catholic Priest for size. The good father had come to Regina for a meeting on Tuesday night. At 2:30 Tuesday afternoon, somebody did something wrong at the corner of Rose St. and 12th Ave. I don't know the details, but Fathers's blue Buick did lose its left front corner. There was the Buick Sales and Service sign about fifty feet from the accident.

The investigating officer, Sergeant Ed Yantz, was also a Buick owner. He simply came in the door and called for the tow truck. At 3:00 p.m., I was working on the blue Buick. Mr. CA Smith, our service manager, was doing a great job of public relations. He and the large priest were having a laughing visit beside the car in my stall. It seemed that there would be no problem at all, as long as the car looked like new, and would have its owner in Winnipeg in time for a parish meeting at 9:00 p.m., the next night.

As I removed the damaged things, the parts pick-up truck came with the new pieces.

Our boss, or president I should say, JB Sangster had recently given a luncheon talk at his club. As a cute little dig to his medical friends, he said, "If you gentlemen were to meet some Israelite that Moses led out of Egypt, you would have no trouble treating that patient. They had the same bodies that we have today. I have a hundred people on staff that have to be smarter than doctors. They have to spend hours of study every month to keep abreast of the changes in the auto service industry." JB went on, "Every year there is a change in style. Every year brings new problems, new ills, new diagnoses, new cures."

It did not take long for the impact of the talk to filter back to us in the work department. In fact, the first we heard of it was that same afternoon when a doctor drove in to get a door adjusted on his Buick. He wanted to know how he could get as smart as all of us auto body men and

95

painters. He found it hilarious. I suppose that was because he had such an easygoing personality, and a keen sense of humour.

Most of us staff members belonged to the General Motors Technicians Guild. We sent in exam papers every month. Oh sure, we were professionals, but we did not class ourselves near the medical people. JB's joke was just a joke.

A bit before ten o'clock that night, the blue Buick was in the paint shop and Elmer was going to get it painted and dried for the road the next day.

At 2:30 Wednesday afternoon, Father was there for his car. It was ready! After a close examination, he thanked us. No he congratulated us on our fast efficient service. This man just emanated friendliness and yet, rigid exactness. With a firm hand shake, the good gentleman was off in a rush for home. The day continued, as they usually do.

Thursday 9:00 a.m., the service manager's phone rang. "Good Morning Charlie, this is Father calling from Winnipeg."'

"Hello Father, how are you?"

"Oh, I am fine, now that I have had time to relax."

With real concern Mr. Smith asked, "What happened Father? Is there something wrong?"

"I was near Portage La Prairie, when I turned on my lights last night. For a second they lit up the whole countryside then went out." He went on, "I got it corrected, and was only ten minutes late for my meeting, so tell that kid that worked on my car, that I forgive him." When the conversation was ended, I was confronted by Mr. CA Smith.

"You were sure lucky to not be in Portage last night."

"Why?" I asked.

"Father would have given you the Last Rights, then tramped you right into the ground."

Again, "Why?"

"You big dumb nut, you put six volt seal beams in a 12 volt system!"

My ego did not get a boost.

The Babysitter

We were married in August. Not many months later, Berniece's cousin, Bob, showed up at our apartment. He was a member of the Royal Canadian Mounted Police, and was sent to F Division training depot in Regina. Before spring graduation, he spent many evenings at our place. Bob was so entertaining, it was a pleasure to have him as a dinner guest. In June he was a full-fledged Mountie and posted to Alberta.

Five years later I got a better job opportunity so, with our two daughters, we moved to Alberta. By that time, Cousin Bob had served the required number of years in the force that allowed him to take a wife.

His choice was a vivacious girl with dark hair, a beautiful complexion and a winning personality. Picturesque is too weak a term to describe Bob and Nat's wedding. The setting was Blairmore Alberta, in the Crows Nest Pass. The white church was guarded by towering green Spruce trees. The groom and three attendants in their dress uniforms, entered the church, which gave an abundance of colour. Men in Scarlet from far and wide had come to the wedding. Add to this, Natalie in her white bridal dress - what a picture!

We, being relatives of the groom, were escorted next to the front pew on the right side of the church. Our girl Margaret age four sat with proper decorum between myself and Berniece. Carolyn, age three, was restless. She eventually crawled on her hands and knees along the polished pew. The place was crowded, all but the end of our pew. At consecration, (the most solemn point of the Mass) the altar bell was jingled and from the far end of our pew and a loud chant filled the entire building. We heard "Its Howdy Doody Time." It was about time for the kids favourite T.V. show. It did give a bit more spark to the after party, much to her mother's embarrassment.

The newlyweds settled in, two blocks from us. To the delight of the girls, we often saw Nat and Bob.

That was the year that the St. Lawrence seaway was being built. That was also the year that General Construction was awarded the contract to rebuild runways at the airport. The seaway job had absorbed

97

all of the heavy tandem drive trucks General Motors had made. Somehow, our sales department combed all of Canada and got nine trucks for the construction company.

The building that we serviced these monsters in, covered part of a city block. I worked next to the entrance door. The four-mile haul of gravel from the river to the runways was hard on these vehicles.

Our girls had been asking for Bob and Nat to come for an evening. On a Tuesday afternoon, when I got home from work, I was informed that we were going to the show at the Paramount. The girls were ecstatic, "Nat and Bob are coming to see us." To the kids, Bob and Nat were not babysitters, they were guests.

The show was over, we went home and the girls were in bed. After coffee and a snack, Bob and Nat were at the front door.

"Thanks for looking after the kids for us."

"It was a fun evening for us," was Nat's answer.

"Tomorrow will be interesting. We are going to run a safety check on General Construction," Bob causally mentioned before he said, "Good Night."

"Goodnight," Now, why in heck did Bob let that remark slip out? I pondered that until I fell asleep.

First thing Wednesday morning as soon as the big door was open, here came Jack, General's gruff, no nonsense, gear jamming, truck boss.

"Say Jack, I heard that they are going to run a safety check on your company to day."

"Where'd ya hear that?"

"From our baby sitter," I answered.

Jack must have ignored my warning. Right after noon, General trucks came rolling in. Signal lights broken, light wires ripped off, windshields cracked, door locks rattled apart. Yes, that trail from the river bottom was hard on these trucks. The time lost was costly for the construction company. They were not pleased at all, especially Jack.

At closing time, Jack checked out their last truck. I had just locked my toolbox when he paused, looked at me and asked, "Who is your baby sitter?"

"Oh, we get an RCMP constable to come over."

"A Mountie baby sitting? What the hell kind of kids do you raise?" Shaking his head in wonder, he kept on his way.

Goldie

The Five Roses Flour sign is no longer there above the door. The old flour shed and I are all that remain of the incident that took place fifty years ago. It was on the second day of my ride home from the southwest that I stayed overnight in town at the house where we now live. I may have bragged a bit about the beauty of my new four year old saddle horse that I had named Goldie. In the morning Aunt Edna said that I should stop in at the house on my way home so she could see this animal.

At the barn I met Hank and he said that my horse had been fed and that all she needed now was some riding. I eased the saddle pad onto her back, this brought no response so next came the saddle loosely cinched. I led Goldie to the water trough, and while she was sipping water, I recalled the last two days of travel. The first afternoon that I had this horse it was a tossup whether I would ride the ninety miles home, or walk leading the mare. We only made twenty miles that day. Every two or three miles, Goldie would try to dissolve our partnership. I figured that she was not too well broke and wanted to go back to her home. As the day wore on the bucking spasms grew less violent and I grew more confident.

On the second day, there was just one minor explosion when I swung into the saddle. The rest of the day was simply great. The horse finished drinking and I finished my reverie about the same time. To be bucked off out on the prairie would have been bad enough, but to be unloaded right in front of the livery barn with onlookers would have been too embarrassing. I tightened the cinch and got deep and snug in the saddle. As we rode away, my horse acted perfect. We jogged the five blocks and turned into Aunt Edna's back yard. I dismounted and held the reins while we posed for a couple of shots from the Kodak 120 box camera. While Aunt Edna, who had ridden some snaky ponies in her day, petted Goldie and scratched her neck, I untied my parka from the saddle and slipped it on.

Gathering the long braided reins, I swung into the saddle. While we finished our visit, I tucked the reins around the horn and between my thigh and the pommel, my gloves were pushed down in front of me. Saying good bye to my aunt, I cued Goldie with a knee to turn out the gate and go to the right. I was busy tying up my parka hood. The horse took just a few dainty steps up the alley toward the rear of Wilkinson's Grocery Store, and there I was, laying on my back in the gravel with my fingers still on the parka strings.   There was a little gray fur ball laying beside or under me, and a white stocking sorrel leg and hoof above us. Goldie took off and went into Wilson's back yard. I jumped up and with a sudden fit of real mad, took after Jack Wilkinson's dog. This pet, with lots of long, curly, gray hair, was about the shape of a loaf of bread, only a bit longer and higher. It had never gotten a swift kick because no one would kick a dog in the head. On this little guy both ends looked the same. I was angry, and the rate of speed the dog was going, it was not hard to tell which end was which. I was handicapped with parka, angora chaps and riding boots. Those boots had the old style underselling solid leather heels, the kind that would plow a pair of furrows in the dirt when you had an animal lunging on the end of a lariat rope. They also jarred your spine on hard ground. Well this ground was hard but my aim was to jar a small animal's spine.

The race was fast and short. It ended at the flour shed. Jack was ready to take the one big step to the ground with a hundred pound bag of flour on his shoulder. The gray poodle, darting at full speed between his feet, caused Jack to stumble and drop the bag. I skidded to a stop at the edge of the white circle of flour on the ground. He looked at me rather upset and fairly shouted, "Why are you chasing my dog? Look at the bag of flour. It's completely ruined."

My answer was about as soft as his question, "Your blankety, blank dog bit my horse in the heels and got me bucked off."

Aunt Edna came leading my horse, with her old box camera in the other hand. The look on her face showed that she was ready to burst with laughter. It ended amiably after she gave us her spectators view of the episode. We all saw the funny side, but the darn dog was still in the flour shed when I rode away.

Hagen's Horses

Hagen had homesteaded south of the trail leading west from Penn, Saskatchewan. The tracks, not a real road, left the Chitek trail north of Blair's. It followed the highest land through the spruce forest, across the narrow neck of muskeg to higher ground again. In this manner, the trail wound its way past Hagen's farm and to the Pelican Reserve.

Hagen was a bachelor. As a young man, he had emigrated from Norway. One afternoon in March, he was hauling a sleigh load of fire wood home. Passing the Spruce Creek school he called, "Yonny, could I give you a ride?"

With Johnny perched up on the aspen logs, holding his book and lunch pail, they moved along. One step now and one step then. The poor horses were old, thin and tired.

"Tomorrow I am going to a sale. I sure would like to buy the team of Percheron mares. Trouble is, they are worth more than three hundred dollars. I only got ninety bucks," Hagen explained to his young friend.

At the sale, Hagen with his fur cap, coat and mitts, was noticeable. Household things were being auctioned first. Hagen would put in a very loud bid on some item that he did not want and knew he would not get for that price. When the auctioneer would turn his way to get that second bid, there was Hagen scooting across the yard, his doggy old coat tail flapping in the wind. He went up over the corral rails and in to inspect the horses. Back at the sale area he would give another loud bid, then back to the horses. This manoeuver was repeated time and again. Hagen was certainly noticed. Before the auctioneer got to the livestock, everyone knew that this old geezer was different. But the team of gray mares also knew Hagen. At long last, the auctioneer was up on the corral with one arm around the gatepost.

"Now, gentlemen! Here we have a pair of Percheron mares, full sisters! Four and five years old. Perfectly matched, broke to drive."

Hagen had his jack knife in his hand, cleaning a hoof. Letting the hoof down Hagen hollered "I'll give you fifty bucks," then went back to digging in a rear hoof. The talking salesman up on the coral, went on to point out the great quality of the mares. Hagen dropped the foot he had been scratching with his knife.

"I'll give you sixty bucks."

In time the auctioneer had run out of good things to say about the team.

"If they are that good, I'll give you ninety bucks," Hagen shouted.

Knowing that he had to begin sooner or later, he started his pitch. "Ninety I have. Who will make it a hundred? Ninety, ninety, ninety, ninety. Ninety." Hagen held his breath. So did the rest of the guys.

Two days later Hagen was hauling wood. At the school, he stopped to give his friend a ride. Johnny sat up on the load. Horse hooves and snowballs just a flying.

"How do you like my new horses, Yonny? Nobody bid, everybody thinks I'm crazy, so I might pay five hundred bucks. I sure will farm faster with my new horses."

Bear Scare

WARNING DO NOT USE THIS IDEA TO PROTECT LIFE OR LIMB. (It has not been approved by Environment Canada). Tom Strang and his partner were young men, prospecting for minerals in northern Ontario. Tom told his story:

"We beached the canoe, and set up camp for the night. After so many hundreds of miles of paddling, we had our system worked out. We set up the tent, and spread our sleeping bags. Next we built the fire pit. This was ground scraped to bare earth then a ring of stone was placed to hold the cooking grill above the fire. With the fire burning down, I would make our supper while Howard put the canoe up out of harms way. Or more exact, out of porcupines way. He would tie a thin rope on each end and pull it up in a couple of trees. He would also pack in the canoe anything that we would not use at this camp. When you are miles out in the wilderness and it is only the canoe that will get you out, you learn to take really good care of it.

I had bacon and sliced potato on the grill, so I took the fly spray and fogged the inside of the tent. While I closed the tent flap, I heard a sound at the fire. Howard is through already? I went over to the fire pit, in deep thought. "Say Howie, should we ------." Looking up, there I was, face to face with a large black bear. He was ready to help himself to some bacon.

Nose to nose we were about three feet apart. Without time to panic, I gave him a quick pump with the spray. He got the bug stuff right in the face. I know that it did not blind him, but he turned and crashed through the trees like he was crazy.

Years later, we were in Yellowstone Park. We were strolling in the evening and because the insects were so bad I had an aerosol can of repellent in my hand. As we rounded some trees there was a huge grizzly bear rummaging in someone's garbage. A woman with her camera was urging her boy and girl to stand on each side of the bear, so all three would pose for the picture.

With my heart in my throat, I ran past the woman, up to the bear and pressed the jet on the aerosol can. Well, that bear forgot about the free meal. He turned and ran straight up the side of the mountain, and kept on going. The old gal was standing by her New York licensed Cadillac and she was fuming.

"You busy body! You scared the bear just when we wanted the picture."

I said, "Lady, are you stupid? That bear could kill each one of your kids with a swipe of each paw."

"But he would not do that. He must be a tame park bear that they have to photograph."

"Go and ask the park people about that," was all I could say to the dizzy dame. "I do not know if it is the smell or the sound of the spray that puts the fear of the devil into bears but, it worked twice for me," was Tommy's summary of the idea.

One evening I was with uncle David while he was feeding his half-grown pigs, and I told him Tommy's story.

"I think that is all it is, too, just a story." Uncle said.

The pigs had come in through the hole cut in the wall, between two studs. The entrance was about two feet square. There were about forty young hungry porkers just gobbling up grain from the long trough.

"A pig is supposed to be somewhat like a bear" Uncle reasoned, "Watch this." Grabbing the insecticide sprayer that held about a quart of fly spray, he vigorously started spraying the pigs at their trough.

Pandemonium broke loose. Forty pigs all tried to get out through the two-foot hole at the same time. When the end of the building stopped squeaking, Uncle Dave said, "Well I'll be darned."

"Yup, me too," I agreed.

Home

We live in a frontier town. The houses and businesses have no numbers. The streets and avenues have names, but they are kept secret in the town's office safe. The people all have names. Some had numbers too. The Military people remember their numbers. The others kept their numbers a secret upon release.

Our frontier town has no passenger trains, no hotel, no bus depot. There are many things our town does not have. We did have five livery barns, a Chinese laundry that hosted high stake poker games and a bar room that sold hard liquor in small glasses. Father time stole all these from us.

Oh, we still have a bar room, but the patrons don't wear spurs.

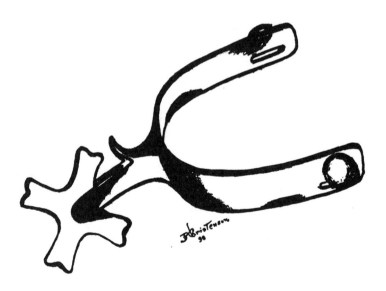

Saskatoon Berries

The spring of 1942 was as dry as it had been for the previous ten years. The crops were mostly all seeded. The old men and those with obligations would shake their heads and mutter, "What's the use." Then it was rain and sun on alternate days. Optimism grew, pasture grass grew, grain crops grew and the berries grew.

I was able to spend most of the summer with Uncle Ted, Aunt Pauline and their four girls and Uncle Dave. They were farming about twenty-five miles east of Calgary. On Sunday morning Uncle Ted brought in the pail of milk.

"I know where there is a good place to look for berries, shall we go?" This was said while he poured the milk into the hand-crank cream separator. Aunt Pauline phoned their neighbour, Mrs. Skibstad, and within minutes a berry picking trip was organized.

In the cab of Uncle Dave's truck besides him were, Pauline, infant Doreen and Mrs. Skibstad. In the box of the truck there were the Skibstads, Norma, Vern, Eric, and Bob, Uncle Ted and his three girls, Doug Robins and myself. We shared the space with pails, boxes, lunch containers, extra sweaters and jackets. That little 1936 Chev half-ton was loaded for berries. We travelled south to the Bow River. At the ranch gate Doug was elected to get out and open and close it. Doug voted "no, "but nine yeses shouted him down.

Two more miles and we were on the Flats. The truck may still have been moving when Uncle Ted was out and said, "C'mon, Bernie." The area where we stopped was a grassy clearing bounded on the east by a stand of aspens that stretched both north and south for some distance. Beyond the aspens was the dense growth of willow. Uncle Ted was crashing through these willows and I was only a half a crash behind. We partly stepped and slid down a four-foot bank and were in semi-open pasture.

"Now, the first thing you do is to find a landmark that you can see from any direction. That way you can get back to the truck any time you wish." With that he was gone hunting a berry bush. Well, there it

107

was, a giant old cottonwood stump about fifteen feet high. Years ago it had lost its bark and now it stood white and naked except for the limb pointing west that supported the huge hawk's nest. Now, that was a land mark, hardly another just like it in all of Alberta. Well, at least not one so close that it would get me lost.

In a half hour we had all been exploring the berry patch, at least one hundred acres of it. Then we went back to the truck for lunch.

"Let's go and get them. They are all prime berries." You couldn't beat Uncle Ted's enthusiasm. During the afternoon the crew was organized like a grazing herd of cattle, wandering here and there. You would talk to someone for a while, then as other berries beckoned, you would move on and meet someone else. Uncle Dave and I were close together when Aunt Pauline and Mrs. Skibstad walked by. Aunt Pauline summed it up, "Prime berries sure, but we will have to go miles to get them."

I rather avoided the two ladies. They were serious berry pickers, consequently, Mrs Skibstad had but a glance of me, the nephew, from Saskatchewan.

We all had one more taste of the lunch. The sun had not touched the horizon so back to the pasture for more wild fruit. It was near dusk when everyone seemed to be in the area of the willows, but far north of the truck.

We all trooped south to a hillside. "No, this is too far." We turned and went back to the starting point. We then marched back to the hill, then back north. .Uncle Ted and Mrs. Skibstad were the leaders. Norma and I fell in step at the rear of the procession.

Norma was a year younger than I, a pretty and vivacious girl. On a one-half hour acquaintance there is not much of a romantic attachment, but we did have many things in common. We were nearing the old cottonwood.

Norma said, "Oh, I wish we could find the truck. I am getting tired of this walking."

Just a few steps more and there was the spot that Uncle and I had dug our heels in on our first trip. "The truck is right here." I climbed the bank and reached a hand to Norma. Seconds later we were at the truck.

Aunt Pauline was there tending baby Doreen. As she handed us lemonade, she asked, "What in heaven's name are those people doing?"

"Oh, I think they are lost," said Norma with no great degree of concern.

From the north, Mrs Skibstad called, "Norma."

The echo had not died when Uncle Ted called, "Bernie."

Aunt put a finger to her lips to ask for silence. The troop went right on by. They turned again at the hill and came back. The leaders were repeatedly calling our names, but with a lot more vigour. In fact they sounded belligerent. They were getting near when Aunt Pauline gave the signal for us to answer. Norma gave out a weak pitiful, "Mom." I heard a gasp for breath and a snort from people in the willows.

As loud as I could, I shouted, "Hello." They heard me. They were less than forty feet away. As they came out of the trees, Mrs. Skibstad gave me a cool look where I sat thirty feet from the truck, then at her cute daughter sitting over by the truck with her back to the fender. Then she gave Aunt Pauline an embarrassed grin.

Uncle Ted grumped, "You could have shouted or blown the horn when we were lost down there."

Aunt could barely hide the mischief in her voice when she answered, "It sounded to me like you were rounding up a herd of elephants down there, and I sure wasn't going to be the one to stampede them."

Buying Bob

"Buying Bob was the best horse deal I ever made. He became the most reliable school pony you could ever wish for. After he got to know his job, I would hitch him to the buggy and he would go two miles to school and get the kids, and bring them home."

"What was he like Grandpa?" I asked.

"He was a small buckskin with a black mane and tail. The black line went along his back from his mane to his tail." Grandpa continued, "I bought him from a Sioux in southeast Montana for ten dollars."

"A few years before that, there were a couple of real tough guys in town that were going to have a shoot out. After supper I had the milk pail on my arm on the way to milk our cow. I was just lighting my pipe when I stepped around the corner of the house and bumped square into one of these tough guys. He had his Colt six gun in his hand. It was such a shock to me, that I hit him on the chin and knocked him out. I took his gun and dropped it in the well. I watched him crawling on his hands and knees, hidden by the railroad grade. He was going out of town. Then I had to go back to the house for another match. My pipe had gone out.

The fall after that, Grandma, Martha and I went up the track on my hand car, to pick wild plums in a coulee. The little place we stopped at was on my section of the railroad, so I put the hand car on the side track, and we went to pick plums. We were just a short way out of town when the deputy sheriff came galloping on his horse."

"Have you got a gun with you?" he hollered.

"No, I left my gun at home."

"Well, I can't let you out of town if you're not armed."

"I'm not looking for trouble. I don't need a gun."

"You have to have a gun in case the range cows surround you."

"There were only the deputy's office, a saloon and the general store. I guess there were a few shacks back near the creek, but that was the whole town. I went to the store and asked for the cheapest gun he had. The storekeeper took a gun off of the shelf and said, "There it is, a a Hopkins and Allan .38 five shot. It, and a box of 50 shells will cost you six bucks.""

As the breeze rustled the leaves on the maple tree that was shading our bench, my seven-year-old ears were craving more of the story.

"I bought the gun and we went out and picked wild plums. When our pails were full, I put the hand car back on the rails and pumped all the way home."

"That country, with its gunfighters, range cows and lawless people got to be too much for me. It was a year later when we were going back to Dakota to homestead. I had three wagons loaded with stuff. We had five guys to take the wagons and horses and cattle to eastern North Dakota."

"Our trail outfit was just about ready to leave when a few Indians rode in and wanted to sell a horse for ten dollars. I bought the thin buckskin pony and sent him east with the rest of the stock. The Indian was a renegade that did not go to Canada with Sitting Bull, but he and a small bunch lived up along the Yellowstone River. They spent the ten dollars on rum. By the time they sobered up, my horses were away over past Roosevelt's ranch, and that was one hundred and fifty miles away.

The section foreman that was taking over my job told me that the Indian was here and was looking for his horse. I got my gun and two of the track crew boosted me up in the attic of a spare bunkhouse. I laid on my stomach across the two-by-fours that the ceiling was nailed to. I had the .38 revolver in both hands with the muzzle right at the trapdoor hole. It was not comfortable but I didn't want trouble.

In time, the searchers got to the bunkhouse where I was hiding. One guy would stand with his hands clutching his knees, while the one that sold me the horse would use the other guy's shoulders to stand on while he checked out the attic. The face with black braids and brown eyes popped up about eight inches from the end of my gun. For a long time he just stared, and did not blink. I didn't blink either. He dropped down from the trap door hole. He and his buddies got on their horses and galloped away to their hide out along the Yellowstone. That was the only thing that gun was ever good for.

We called the pony Bob. He took the kids to school hitched to the buggy or sleigh. At school in the morning, they would send him home. At three o'clock I would hook him up and he would go to school and get the kids. Bob took your aunt Anna, aunt Emma, uncles Emil, Reinhart, Albin, George and your Mom to school.

We came to Canada, but Bob was too old to make the trip. He stayed in Dakota."

Today's only link with this episode, is my memory of Grandpa's story and the .38 revolver.

Old Bones

It had been a long steady drive. The gas gauge read low. Miles of flat desert stretched away to the blue-black mountain peaks just visible over the sage. There, beside the narrow, pitted highway, sat a little country store with gas pumps in front.

I got out of the truck and stretched the kinks out of my back and legs. I filled the truck with gas and turned to go in and pay for it.

I paused when a voice said, "With that license plate you got, you are a long way from home." It came from an old man sitting in a rocking chair.

"Well, every hour I get a little bit closer," I replied. The screen door squeaked when I went in. I paid the white-haired lady and asked, "Have you a lost cowboy sitting out in the shade?"

"Oh, that's mah husband, you could cawl him that."

"Would he mind having a Coke with me?"

"If you can stop and set a spell, he'd love it." This was said in the voice and accent of the old southwest.

I bought two Cokes and the screen door squeaked again. He thanked me for the drink and introductions were easily taken care of. He moved a backless kitchen chair out with a scuffed boot toe and invited me to, "Hep yourself." We sat under the roof that extended from the side of the store.

"What part of Saskatchewan do you hail from?" he asked, nodding toward the plate on my front bumper.

"Down toward the south west corner," I answered.

"I was pretty young when I helped move some cows from the Missouri River up to the Cypress Hills. We crossed the Milk River and followed along a small river in Canada. Now, what was that name?"

"Oh that would be the Frenchman," I said, trying to help his memory.

He shook his head, "No, I don't recollect that name."

"Maybe it was the White Mud?"

113

"Yup, that was her. We trailed along on the south side for a day or two, crossed the little river about where they dug up the dinosaur." His memory was searching back through the years.

This man was many shades of gray, his old rolled-brim Stetson, blue-gray eyes, gray shirt, and blue jeans, faded gray. The only contrast was his brown face and sinewy wrists and hands.

"You heard about that Rex Dinosaur they found in Saskatchewan?"

"Yes, it is about eighty miles from home where they are digging up them old bones," I answered.

"That big old lizard was not a native guy the way I see it. A long time ago the Gulf of Mexico come dern near to West Texas." With that, he stood up. Reaching into his pocket, he got out his jackknife. Seated again, he tested the knife edge on his thumb. Picking up a foot-long chunk of a tree branch, he took a perfunctory shave off of the stick (this guy was loaded with self assurance).

"Yes sir, it was a long time ago. That line about a big bang killing off the dinosaurs ain't even eye wash. Same thing as what happened to that Rex guy in Canada." The ever so thin whittling was coming off the branch.

When I was a kid, I saw whittlers. Uncle and a bull buyer each whittled a pile of shavings before they cinched the price of the bull. This old fella was a whittler.

"Now this Rex fella had finished a good feed and was lying on the beach sunnin' himself. What woke him up was the granddaddy of all earthquakes. Well, it just rumbled and roared and shook for more than ten days. That was when them Sierra Mountains in Mexico, the Daves here in Texas and that chain that runs up into New Mexico was pushed right up out of the bowels of the earth. Mile high hot rocks was all that was left of his old home pasture. Well, under those conditions old Rex had to move on."

"Down along here someplace, he got filled up on sage. Now that is no good for a meat-eating animal. To get away from the volcanic heat and smell, he wandered on north. In Colorado he took on a big feed of pine needles. It was the only green thing he had seen for days. That made him sicker'n a dawg. He limped along with this terrible indigestion. He made poor time across Nebraska and South Dakota. The sand was wearing the hide off the underside of his tail. Travel was slow and painful."

My dinosaur exponent took another grip on the stick and kept right on whittling those thin slices of wood. "By this time he had lost so much condition that you could count his ribs. He cut in, west of the Black Hills. Somewhere in Montana he came to a bunch of fern type plants. He cleaned up that little meadow in no time. The pain and rumbling in his stomach eased up, but that was no food for a beast that size to travel on."

The pile of whittlings was growing. "Yes sir, he finally came to the White Mud. He had a big drink and laid down out of the wind and hoped to soak up a little sunshine. Well, he laid down and had a peaceful sleep. His last one. He never did wake up."

About this time the razor-sharp knife blade had whittled so close to his left thumb that I was relieved to have old Rex laid to rest.

Black Powder

It was a bright summer afternoon when our neighbours, Mr. and Mrs. Walker, dropped in for a visit. Charles and I had gone for a coffee refill. Our wives had hurried out to the raspberry patch. The conversation leading to the point where we will join it, was too desultory to try to recapture.

"My Grandparents lived in Montana before the turn of the century," I mentioned.

"Mine were in Minnesota about the time they were getting the boundaries sorted out." Charles said and then continued, "My great-grandfather bundled up his family at Quebec City and moved south. There, they joined a group of settlers going west to find new land. Finding suitable soil in Minnesota, they stopped and built a fort. The fort had high stockade walls with a tower at each corner. All the people of the community lived within these walls. At night the livestock were also secured in the fort.

About that time, several young Indian men at Pine Ridge Dakota Territory, got a bit bored with life. It all started so simply. These guys were lounging under a twisted pine tree on a hillside above the main camp.

"You know fellas the white people have built another fort over east."

"Ya, I heard that it is about an eight-sleep trip to get over there."

"Oh, I think it would take longer than that. It's on the far side of the north and south water(Mississippi). It is supposed to be on level land, south of the lakes and hills."

"Maybe we should take our rifles and ride over that way."

"If we just go hunting, we could get to the shallow crossing of the Missouri, then we would be out of range of the cavalry so they couldn't send us home here to the reservation."

"I bet we can find some kind of fun over there." That was the whole plan. These guys were not a war party, just a handful of young fellows out for a good time, and maybe a scalp or two.

To the west of the fort was the hay meadow. To the right of that was the small patch of developed field where the corn and potatoes were growing. Farther to the right of the meadow was the grassland where Charles' Grandfather herded all the cattle of the settlement. Being twelve years old, Master Walker had the herder's job. He took pride in that job, and did it well.

The hay had been cut by hand with scythes. The sweep of the long slim blade was controlled by the harvester's right hand on the curved handle. With his left hand, the distance of the blade from the ground was governed. The haymaker would position himself at an angle to the edge of the field, then a mighty swing of the scythe, a two by three-foot strip of hay was cut. Step swing, step swing, step swing and that was the routine that was used until the hay field was cut. After the required drying time, the hay was raked into piles. This was done with a handmade tool, much like a modern garden rake, the difference being in the width, and they were made of wood from the nearby forest. The size of the rake depended on the size or energy of its owner. These operations were followed by coiling. This was a matter of forking the hay into round mounds that would be about four feet high. The building of the hay mounds, or cocks as they were called, allowed them to shed rain and complete the curing process.

Before daylight, the Indian boys from Pine Ridge had hid their ponies in the tall trees on the side of the meadow across from the stockade. A while after sunrise, Master Walker signalled that he had the cattle ready to take to the grazing area. "Open the gate," he called. Within minutes he had the stock hungrily eating the lush grass.

A sentry on the parapet thought that he saw a haycock on the far edge of the field move. This is not possible. Haycocks don't move. Ridicule or not, he quietly pointed out his suspicion to his fellow guard. Careful watching, and sure enough, there were six or seven haycocks on the far edge of the field, all inching their way toward the fort. Master Walker was the only person outside of the stockade! The bugle note was warning enough. The kid done a hurry up gather of the stock and had

117

them heading back to the fort. That was, all but the spotted bull, who was not a massive animal but old enough to be grumpy. Instead of going home he charged the herder. Walker dropped to one knee, aimed the muzzle loading gun and fired. With a BANG the black powder exploded leaving a cloud of gray white smoke at the end of the gun barrel. The bull fell on its side, shot in the head. The rest of the cattle and their herder were soon safe within the stockade.

A few rifle balls sent in the direction of the far haycocks let the Indians know that their plan had kind of gone haywire. If they did shoot from under the haycocks, it would have been impossible to reload. To pour in the black powder and ramrod in the rifle ball was out of the question. They crawled from under the haycocks and took shelter in the nearby forest. It was certainly discouraging to have ridden across two territories and have things go so wrong so early in the day. The Dakota gang could only shoot high above the fort and feel pride when the odd ball would even reach the walls of the fort. The defenders were not plainsmen with years of warfare behind them, nor did they have the best of rifles for long range shooting. Now and then, they would fire a shot toward the guys in the forest. This was rather a dull war being fought, but nerves were taught in the stockade. Indian attacks were generally a mighty serious problem.

When it comes right down to facts, neither the attackers nor the defenders could shoot worth sour apples at that distance. The Indians wanted to save what little ammunition they had, so in the late afternoon they started on their way home. People in the fort wanted to save their shot and powder too, they liked the turn of events. Since just after sunrise there had been guns booming.

Pour a measure of black powder in the muzzle of the rifle, then the grease patch and ball, ram it in tight with the hickory ramrod, replace the ramrod in its holder under the gun barrel, thumb back the hammer, put a cap on the nipple, aim and fire. The intended victim could tell when a shot was fired. When the charcoal, sulfur and saltpeter that made up the black powder were fired, it always gave a telltale cloud of white smoke along with the bang. The quiet of twilight was a welcome relief from the noise of the day.

A keen guard was in order. Maybe the main band would attack at any time. Well after dark, there was a bellering commotion outside the fort gate. The bull had come home with one horn shot off. Having had a big taste of black powder, he must have played possum in the grass until he figured it was safe to come home."

Braddock

Braddock was a growing town, with a community hall and a general store. The railroad was only a couple years away. Surely with such a location it would grow. The town site was high, dry and level with plenty of room to expand. Parker's General Store and Post Office was the economic and social center of town.

The Royal Canadian Mounted Police were sure there was a still operating in the gravel hills to the north east of the new hamlet. By logic alone, Braddock was under suspicion. A clue that a still had been used was not enough to build a court case on.

Two police officers met a local lady, who had just traded in seven pounds of farm churned butter on her grocery purchase, less than a mile west of town. These officers had orders to search Braddock because it was so close to where the sinful still had been used. To search Braddock amounted to tying their horses and having a look through Parker's Store. Upon entering the store, the officers introduced themselves and explained the purpose of their visit.

Mr. Parker pointed out that they had no reason to search his building and, furthermore, they were not welcome.

"Sir, here is our search warrant! We will search every inch of this place." The police made this statement in a cold official voice.

Mr. Parker grabbed a double-bitted axe from the wall and ran to stand on the trap door leading to the cellar under the store. In a mood of righteous indignation, the store keeper was swinging the axe and shouting, "YOU HAVE NO RIGHT. YOU HAVE NO REASON. YOU GOT NO BUSINESS HERE. I DON'T WANT YOU HERE. GO AWAY!" The poor man became incoherent and exhausted at about the same time. At that point, the officers tried persuasive reasoning.

Mr. Parker had to give in. "Oh well, all right. If you must, you must. Give me a hand to move the butter tub." The police each took a handle of the big round wash tub with its lumps of ice and seven pounds of butter, each with its white wrapper with blue printing. Sliding the tub to the side, the cops lit their lantern, lifted the trap door and went down the ladder.

The few guys sitting around the store were quiet and solemn. Mr. Parker, who was perched on a stool behind the counter, looked very upset. His breathing was deep and steady and his nostrils were still flaring. This scene did not change in the next half hour. At long last the searchers emerged from the cellar, each taking a cursory glance over the shelves of merchandise.

"We are finished. Good day, Mr. Parker."

With a coarse laugh that contained a sneer, Mr Parker shouted after them, "Come back again when you want to use up another search warrant."

The Mounties rode up the trail to the west. The atmosphere in the store became more relaxed. A lone horseman arrived from the west.

He was greeted by, "Did you see the cops on the road?"

Teddy answered. "Yup, they wanted to know what I was doing. I told them I had been blasting rocks and now I'm going home."

The merchant wanted to know, "Did they keep on going or could they double back?"

Teddy reasoned, "They won't be here today because they'll have to break a sweat on them horses if they hope to make Swift Current tonight."

In the store Mr Parker said, "Come on Teddy, give me a hand to put the butter tub back on the cellar door." With the tub back in place, the store keeper fished his hand around under the ice lumps in the tub and brought out a bottle of clear liquid.

"Look at this! I just found a sample of my special homemade whiskey. Let's have a snort." As an after thought he chuckled, "Pretty good acting, huh?"

Big Brothers

Glen is a big tall rawboned man with a deep voice, handlebar mustache, and gray eyes that fairly light up when he smiles. He looks the part of a Texas Lawman, which he was, years ago. Right after Pearl Harbor, he joined the US Marines who posted him in a west coast city.

Glen, with two other officers, had a strange type of wartime job. They worked in civilian dress, on civilian time and in a civilian locality. This also meant that they didn't have to live on base. To military people this was unheard of good fortune.

The biggest drawback was that there were no places to live available in a port city in wartime. To correct the situation, the three servicemen polished up Glen's 1938 "Special Sport Buick" convertible. Glen did not have the handlebar twirling mustache then, just the fine line of a military officer on his upper lip. He was a handsome, dashing Marine. He and his Buick made a striking pair.

The three rogues dressed in the very best Marine fashion, started to hunt for an apartment. These three were not rogues in the true sense of the word, more like devil- may-care young servicemen. The morning search yielded nothing. Glen was certain that in a place this size, there had to be a better place to live than on base.

The next plan was to canvas the residential section. Late in the afternoon, they came to a luxuriant old house. After rattling the brass knocker, the door was opened by a spry white-haired lady. In answer to the question of vacant rooms, "Definitely not!" she continued, "My seventeen-year-old-grand daughter and I are alone in our house. We would not be able to keep soldiers."

Glen rose to the situation, "She would be the same age as my little sister back in Texas. Glory be! How I miss that kid. This bloody war is such a hardship on so many people. It is terrible for all of us, every person in the entire nation."

Number two Marine caught on fast, "Just a year older than my sister back home in Oklahoma."

It was number three's turn, "I would give everything to be home in Louisiana. I would take my cousin Amy-May with me a fishin'. She's seventeen too."

Glen's turn. "This is not so far from work. We would save a lot of precious gasoline." A pause, "We should go and look somewhere else."

One and Two in unison, "But where? It seems that we have looked everywhere."

The prospective landlady weakened just a wee bit, "Well, maybe."

These three young men saw that they had to appear to be the solid citizens of the generation between Grandma and Granddaughter.

Glen being very humble said, "If you could possibly find room for us for even a week, we will swear an oath that no harm will come to you or your granddaughter in the short time we would be here."

Hesitating still, Grandma said, "Maybe you should see the rooms first." Uncle Sam's three hirelings followed the old lady up the stairs. Examining the second floor she said, "These three bedrooms could be used. The one across from the bathroom, is rather small." She paused, "When will you bring your things?" she asked.

"Could we move some of our clothes today?" Glen asked.

"Yes, if its going to be, you might as well."

The three Marines got into Glen's Buick convertible. Their first idea was to have a big victory bash at the officer's club. On second thought they decided that they had best secure the beachhead. It would be sad to lose the rooms at Granny's house, and have to live in the barracks.

Days later the neighbourhood watchers saw the Buick, Ford and Chev parked in front of Granny's house. Three service men coming or going, but only the same three, and always quiet and polite. If the Marines got wind of the granddaughter going out, one was posted at the upper window. When the swain arrived he was met at the front door by a stiffly dressed Marine officer.

"Where are you young people going tonight?" Upon getting the answer, he would tell, "Now you be very careful, and be home in good time." Patting the girl on the shoulder he would say, "Good night Alice, have a nice time."

A week later a soldier boy showed up. He was intercepted as Alice came from her quarters. A full scale officer was a surprise. Glen said as sharp as could, "ATTENTION!" The recruit snapped to attention. Glen of course returned the salute, but left the poor guy standing ramrod straight with his boot heels one half inch apart.

"Where do you plan on going private?"

"To the dance at our canteen, sir."

"Is that a well-chaperoned function?"

"I, I, I think so, Sir."

Glen gave an icy look. "You must be back here by 11:30. DO YOU HEAR ME?"

"Y-Y-Yes, Sir."

"And furthermore you will bring Alice home as sweet, pure and beautiful as she is now. If not you should get a sidearm, put the muzzle in your ear and fire the gun. It would be much better for you." He gave one more stare and then the command, "At ease."

Glen turned to Alice, with a kind brotherly voice, "Run along now, and enjoy yourselves."

Returning to his buddies, Glen said, "You're darn right Gran heard me. I think we're in here to stay."

Another bit of insurance was to write a letter to a gal in Texas. The instructions were, copy this out word for word and send it back. The answer soon arrived, with an extra page.

Page one: Glen, what the h--- are you up to? Knowing you as the scoundrel you are, I bet it's to no good, signed, Rosie. Losing page one and offering page two Glen said, "Gran, you must read a letter from my sister." Gran read, "Dear Glen. We miss you so much at home, etc., etc." The body of the letter was the usual down home news. The ending that Glen had composed and sent to Texas for the rewrite, read;

> I am so glad you have found such nice people
> to live with. It is what you marines deserve. Alice
> must be a beautiful girl, and Gran is such a sweet lady
> to take you boys in. Say hi to both of them for me.
>
> Love,
>
> Your Sister, Betty

The letter had the right effect. Gran had a thought, "If only things were not so hard to get, and tradesmen so scarce, we could make the small bedroom into a kitchen for you boys."

Marines to the rescue! A bit of skullduggery by Grandma's three roomers, and some plumbers and electricians from the base (who were not above borrowing government pipe and wire to install in a private home), the second-floor kitchen was brought about. The fridge and stove were delivered by an Army-coloured truck after dark.

The tall guy with the handlebar mustache said, "Yes, we stayed in that house for three years. In fact, until we were discharged from the service. Maybe some of our wild youth rubbed off on Grandma, but a lot of Grandma rubbed off on us. To stay on Granny's good side, we raised heck with Alice's love life. We always scared the devil out of all her boy friends."

Passing Through

I stopped my truck and walked over to the corral to join Uncle Sidney. "It's a nice bright morning. It was a good shower of rain we had last night," and all of the good morning type of talk was taken care of. We were leaning with our forearms on the top rail of his bull pen.

To lean just right like that, with your hat brim pulled down to shade your eyes from the morning sun, is something that has to be learned.

"That red bull over by the light roan seems to have an upset stomach," I observed.

"Yeah, he got his head through the fence and ate up all the fresh bromegrass he could reach," Uncle explained. "In a day or so, when he's been back on dry hay, I'll get him in the chute and curry the manure off his back end, before some bull buyer comes to take a look at these animals."

I had stood admiring the dozen or so Shorthorn bulls when Uncle broke the silence.

"Look at that red sucker with the dirty hind end trying to find another place to stick his head through the fence."

Another bull happened to give Dirty Red a friendly bunt in the belly. That put a momentary hump in Red's back and interrupted his search for a spot to stick his head through.

"He still looks a lot better than Will Siever's bull did one time." This statement made me turn my head and adjust my hat brim.

Uncle Sidney remembered, "I had just gotten Virgy, that was the mouse coloured saddle horse I had for years. I was about fourteen at the time. One evening that summer, I rode over to Ekdahl's. Alfred was my age, Hilda. Carl, and Ellen were younger and Oscar was just a little duffer. When I got there, Alfred and Hilda were trying to teach Carl to catch a ball. Mr. Ekdahl was sitting on the front step minding little Oscar. I had put Virgy in the barn and joined in the ball game, when Mr. Siever came along riding one of his work horses bareback.

Charlie Ekdahl was still sitting on the step. Mr. Siever sat on his horse.

"Have you seen my bull?"

Charlie pointed in the direction of the granary, "He's down there."

Mr. Siever went and followed his bull around a few buildings then gave up. He came to ask Alfred and I if we would help him get his bull home.

We got our horses out and went after the bull. Virgy had not been ridden much but she was quick on her feet and of more use than the other two horses put together.

We finally got the bull out on the road and headed south. The ornery cuss sure did not want to go home. If he would have liked being there, he wouldn't have left in the first place. It seemed that the bull had gotten rather worked up by the time he was out on the road. There were thin white strings of slobber trailing from his mouth. He walked with his head low and swinging from side to side. Every few steps he would give a deep throaty grumble. He also swished his tail from side to side and passed manure at the same time. This gave him the round, green, smelly patches where his tail brushed his rump.

Mr. Siever told us boys that was the way the bull always acted when he was angry. The bull had gone a half a mile on the road home. He had only one mile south and one mile east more to go and he would be there. The square mile to the east of the road had no fence on it. (Now, seventy-five years later, there still is no fence on that land.)

The grumpy bull followed by three horsemen came to the curve in the road that edged around the big slough. Everything was going according to plan. The bull was trudging home. The peaceful prairie evening was exploded by a big green-head mallard duck. With a frightened squawk, wild churning of the water and violent beating of the air with its wings, the bird was gone. At the activity of the duck, Siever's horse lifted its head and looked. My horse squatted, stiff-legged in surprise. Alfred's horse thought he should go home so he turned around on the road. What was worse, this all happened very close to the right side of the bull, so he went to the left. The line of travel was a direct path to Mr. and Mrs. Hamilton's house about three hundred yards away.

This was no great mansion, just a comfortable three roomed homestead shack. A door led to the small kitchen with one window on the opposite wall. To the side, there was a living room and a bedroom.

The bull reached the house and proceeded to circle it. At each corner of the house the obstinate beast would turn very close to the wall, still grunting and grumbling and wagging his head from side to side. Mr. Siever, in the few years since he had left Germany, had never had to face a problem like this. "Stay behind me boys," was all he could think of saying. This parade, led by the bull then Siever then myself with Alfred bringing up the rear, soon attracted Mr. Hamilton's attention.

He came through the screen doorway with a dripping paint brush in his hand. Being a man to take command of a situation, and being on a supposedly higher mental plain than most people, he dropped the paint brush and said, "You boys get back, get way back. Siever you go one way and I'll go the other way and we'll soon have that bull going the right way." With that, he reached in the kitchen door and grabbed the broom. He didn't take time to close the door but went hot footing it after the bull going around the house. Sure enough, Hamilton, the bull and Siever all met at the kitchen door. The bull went in the door across the room and freshly painted floor and out the window. He bee-lined straight for home, wearing Hamilton's kitchen window frame for a collar. Me and Alfred bee-lined it home too."

It's Not All Roses

DATELINE, SASKATOON March 18, 1992
"Government cutbacks of 14 percent to urban municipal funding, will cause a ten-dollar increase in property tax to each ratepayer in the city." The person hosting the news conference, ended the interview by saying, "The financial situation we are in is no bed of roses."

VANGUARD, SASK. February 1943. No dateline, no news release, just commonplace conditions. Lloyd and Johanna got the children off to school, then loaded the cream can and crates of eggs in the sleigh. This produce was wrapped in blankets and robes as protection from the cold. It was cold. The ten-mile drive into town was long and chilly. Lloyd drove slowly so his horses wouldn't be warm and sweaty while they had to stand in town.

The cream can was delivered to the train station for shipment to the creamery. The eggs were taken to the store to be bartered for groceries. This was Johanna's department.

Lloyd went to the elevator company, for stove coal. The sleigh box was approximately twelve feet long, three and one-half feet wide and three feet high. He shovelled a couple of ton of coal into the back end of the box. This would leave a place in the front for his wife to huddle under blankets and robes if a blizzard blew in while they were on their way home. Lloyd had more to do in town than Johanna. Load coal, check at the John Deere dealer for parts needed in the spring, nails at the hardware store, pick up the mail and groceries etc. Johanna shopped in the store for the family needs. When this job was complete, it was a short hike down the street and around the corner to her friend Edna's house. Over coffee cups they discussed the record snowfall. Only one car had come to town during the week. All the roads were snowed in. The very few farmers that did not have horses to get around with were in a sorry state.

"Yesterday, did I ever have trouble baking bread," Johanna lamented. "I made eight loaves and put four in the oven. An hour later I was going to take them out and bake the rest. They had just raised a bit more but were not baked at all, so I put more coal on the fire to heat the oven more. Two hours later the bread still had not baked. I had to keep kneading down the other four pans."

Johanna explained how she solved the mystery. "I make a little bit more dough than I need and put a fist size wad in the hole in the corner of the oven where it's rusted out. When the kids went to school, the black tom cat snuck in and ate my patch out of the oven. That was why the oven wouldn't heat up. Well, I was baking bread all day."

Economically, things were not so good. It was no bed of roses then either, except possibly for the black tom cat.

No Change

The winter snow was nearly all gone. It was a warm day with a promise of spring. Frank and Henry were old timers in the district. Frank with his sawmill and Henry with a team of horses, a wagon and a couple of cows, had moved in when the country was opened for settlement.

One morning, I was in town to get the mail. Henry called across the street, "You have time for a coffee? Come on over."

I went into Robin's Nest with them. In the café, we talked of the relief from the cold and the end of a long hard winter.

"And how is the feed holding out?" Henry asked.

"Oh I guess we'll make it, but there won't be much hay left over for next year," was my assessment of the winter.

Our talk went back to other winters, good times and bad were remembered. Frank remembered of waiting for forty below zero weather when he had to split four-foot aspen logs to sell for fire wood.

"When it was so cold that the sap in the logs was froze hard, they would split from end to end with one hit of the axe." That was Frank's memory of the good old days.

"There were two winters that my brother and I contracted to split and load many box cars of fire wood."

With a chuckle, Henry said, "Yes, those were the days. When I came in, I had nothing but a team and wagon, and a couple of cows." Henry continued, "I had no equipment, but the neighbours let me join them at their hay camp. We had a tent set up out in the wilderness. Of course, our homesteads were in the wilderness too. But, that was where we lived and made our hay."

"One day we were out of meat, so I took my 38.55 Winchester and went out for a deer. About a mile from camp I found a young buck with a small set of antlers. I drew a bead on him and fired and down he went. I had only two cartridges left for my rifle, so I laid it down and ran up to bleed the deer. Just as I got there it rose on its hind feet and struck at me with its forefeet. One front hoof slit my jacket, shirt and underwear from my collar to my waist, just as if it was cut with a sharp knife. All I had was a red scratch on my belly. Just think, if it had been an inch closer to me I would have been sliced open and dead before anyone would have found me. I should have shot again but I thought that I should save my shells. A person sure takes some foolish chances at times."

With that Henry signalled to Helen to refill our coffee cups. Two years before, Henry had sold his ranch, and he and his wife moved into town for retirement, but he had kept his trap line.

"Frank, you know where the creek runs into Deer Lake, and up the creek a couple of miles where it is just swamp and willows? Well, last week the snow was getting soft so I left my snow machine and walked in a half a mile to see a mink trap. Would you believe it? I had a wolf in my mink trap. He was only caught by the middle claw on one foot. My rifle was on the machine, and I knew that if I went back for it the wolf would free himself before I could get back. I took a good grip on my little belt hatchet, and crowded the wolf to the end of the trap chain. He eyed me for a moment and sprang, When he was in the air coming at me, I swung the little axe."

I shuddered and thought to myself, "Henry, you old trapper, in all these years, you haven't changed a bit."

"Come over to the garage behind the house, I'll show you guys a darn good wolf pelt," Henry said with a smile.

Big Worry

It was in the late fall, thirty years after Berniece and I were married. I stood at the bedroom window unbuttoning my shirt. On the other side of the glass it was still, quiet, impenetrable black. Not a hint of light, nothing but thick, deep, mysterious dark outside. I was getting ready for bed, but thinking about cows. Looking out to the corrals for a last look at the saddle horses, I could see nothing, it was just plain dark.

Berniece entered the room and exclaimed, "Dear, you have a nasty scratch on your neck, and on this ear too."

"I rode through the west pasture today, looking for cows. Some of those tree branches are sharp," I explained.

"How many are missing?" she asked.

"Counting cows and calves, about thirty head."

She switched off the bed lamp and said goodnight.

With blankets up to my chin I must have muttered out loud, "Those cows must have gotten over to the section eight pasture."

Berniece stirred a bit and mumbled with a yawn, "What did you say? Pardon me. I must be half asleep. I guess I'm like the sleeping doll I had when I was little. When she laid flat, her eyes closed. When I sat her up, her eyes were wide open. I wonder how those dolls worked?"

"Very simple," I explained. "The eyes were two clay marbles joined by a wire that had a lead weight on it. The white, pupil, and iris were painted on and the eyelashes were glued to the marbles. When you laid her down, the weight closed the eyes. When you sat her up, the weight opened her eyes."

"Say how come you know so much about dolls' eyes?" asked my wife.

"Well, when I was a little shaver, I had one of those dolls too. Mom had a straight back rocking chair. One day I was rocking furiously and my dolls head got under the rocker of the chair. Her head got smashed into tiny pieces, but I saved the eyes. I had them in my toy box for years," I assured her.

"What an awful thing to tell me now," my mate stated.

"Why?"

"Because I won't be able to sleep."

"Why?"

Sitting bolt upright in bed she answered, "How do you expect me to sleep with a psychopathic person that smashes sleeping dolls heads, and even saves their eyes in a toy box?" Then she added, "I'll have to sit here all night in sheer terror."

"Goodnight."

"G'nite."

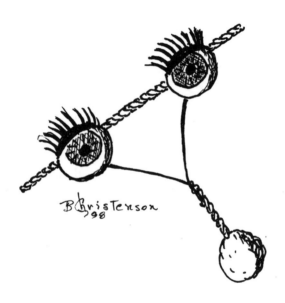

The Sheep Men

On the last day of school, when the last student had been dropped off, Jim was going to cross the highway when a cattle liner wiped off the front of his school bus. I got the job of repairing the bus. Later, Jim came back to the shop and claimed there was a bad rattle in the front of the bus when he drove on rough roads, so we road tested it until we found the problem.

It was ten minutes after noon when we come in from the country and crossed the street where we lived. I swung over and parked the bus in front of our house. We went in to eat. Bernice would set another plate at the table. After meat, vegetables and pie, we sat around the table sipping coffee and chewing on toothpicks.

"Where did you grow up, Jim?" I asked.

"On a sheep ranch in southeastern Alberta." That was the key that unlocked this story.

He continued, "Our family had a large block of pasture in the short grass country of rolling hills and open plains. You wouldn't find a tree in a long day's walk. Father had hundreds of sheep and, at that time, two sheep herders. One was a dark complexioned fellow we called Mex. He was most likely a Spanish Basque herder, or the son of one. That guy thought like a sheep and Dad said he was the best man that ever came to the ranch. The other man was fresh out of England. He was a good worker too, and determined to never make a mistake. His name was Reginald. That was all he ever told us, and that is what we called him, never Reg or Reggie.

Reginald was so polite. Mom claimed he was over polite. He always wore a white shirt and a small black bow tie that he tied himself. I know because, as a little kid, I watched him put it on. A black bowler hat and a long black coat that came nearly to his gray spats that he was never without, made up the rest of his apparel.

In his upstairs room in the old ranch house, his only possession, besides his clothes, was a small locked trunk. He kept his room so spotless that Mother hardly ever went in to check for dirty clothes or lint under the bed. If Reginald was asked about his past, he was so vague that it seemed that his life had started when he landed at the ranch. He would often go off on a dream of his.

"When I have made enough money, I will go back to The British Isles and buy a castle. I will marry a girl, Catherine, and have a son Randolf and a daughter Genevieve. There, the only work I will do is to have conferences with the farmer, the animal husbandry man, the head gardener, the grounds keeper and that sort of help. You know, just to assure myself the estate is well and producing."

We heard this plan time and time again, but we let him have his dream.

One day in the late fall, the sheep men were bringing in a flock of old ewes that Dad was going to sell. Mex and Reginald had a team of horses with some hay on the wagon. This was to help keep these old girls on the trail. There were about three hundred sheep in the band.

They were not too many miles from home, when cold dark clouds blew in from the northwest. The wind got very strong and snow fell so heavily that it swirled on the ground. The snow was driven into the wool and faces of the sheep. Blindly, the old lead ewe swung off the trial to drift with the wind. Just like a signal, the rest of the flock followed her. Reginald hurried to turn them back. Mex shouted for him to come back to the wagon. The storm was so bad that Reginald didn't hear the warning. Even if he had heard, he would have still tried to save the flock.

The weather was so bad that Mex, standing at the front of the wagon box, could not see the heads of the horses. All he could do was huddle in the hay and trust the horses to find their way home. In the morning the storm was not as bad so Dad and Mex took the team and wagon and at first light went out to find Reginald and the lost sheep. About four miles down wind from where Mex last saw them, there were Reginald and the flock of sheep. All had perished in the cold.

The English chap had frozen to death trying to save a hopeless situation. The folks and neighbours had a funeral for him in our church in town and buried him in the cemetery. Days later when Dad went to pay the undertaker, he was handed all of the possessions found on the deceased. There was a folded newspaper clipping of the progress of the

Boer War in Africa. The other item was a small brass key. Mom and Dad used the key on Reginald's trunk.

Of all the things they found, none was as much of a surprise as the old photograph of a castle. Standing with the great door in the background was a man, a woman and a boy and girl. In white writing were the names Earl Reginald, Lady Catherine, Master Randolf and Miss Genevieve."

Jim summed it up, "Here he had the castle and family all the time. Something caused him to mentally snap so he was sent to Canada to save the family name from embarrassment."

Poor Pete

Everyone called him Poor Pete, of course, not to his face, but when he was the subject of the conversation. Poor Pete was not poor financially. In fact, he was wealthier than most of his neighbours. Being a middle-aged bachelor, with a very quiet lifestyle, meant that his money just accumulated in small amounts. Poor Pete was just plain shy, withdrawn and insecure where people were involved. In harvest time or in an emergency, Pete would always help out, but not talk. That was why he was Poor Pete to the neighbourhood.

On his sporadic trips to town where there were people, he kept his eyes focussed seventeen inches in front of his leading foot.

On one such trip to pick up a few groceries and his mail, Poor Pete did a deed that even shocked himself. He absconded with a magazine that was not his. It was dog-eared and smudged. Many unwashed fingers had turned the pages. It had been on the bench in the poolroom when he had sat there to sort his mail.

The old paper which no one seemed to own did have an eye-catching line on the cover. It read, "A New Life for You." The picture was of a lady and man walking away at an angle, a discreet distance apart. All that was visible of the couple were their backs and a slight bit of their right sides. What was different was that they were completely undressed. Poor Pete sort of got the magazine mixed up with his own mail, and snuck it home. He studied it page by page to find out about the "New Life" deal. It seemed to boil down to a promotional script for a sun bathing club.

After months of deliberation Poor Pete sent off a query. He was ready to mail the letter when it occurred to him that it would be wise to not let it be known that he was hunting for a new life. He rewrote the letter, using a general delivery address in the city.   March with its warm winds came, so Poor Pete travelled to the city to check the general delivery counter of the post office. No mail! Our friend went to a show, got a hotel room, and travelled home on Sunday. Two weeks later he repeated the trip. He got his hotel, read his mail and went home in the morning.

The letter was several pages long. The highlights that stuck in Poor Pete's mind were, "Shed your inhibitions," "Be one with nature," "Glory in the power of the sun." It went on for pages. The clincher was, "Any Immoral Act will be the cause of that member being debarred from our community."

"Now that makes sense to me," Poor Pete thought to himself. He threw caution to the wind and made up his mind to join. The address of the club was a long way away. As a precaution, Poor Pete had new tires put on the Chev coupe. Day after day, the little blue car with seventeen inch wheels got him closer to his destination.

Arriving at the right address, Poor Pete parked his car and entered the door marked, 'MEMBERSHIP OFFICE.' With newfound courage Poor Pete was able to answer all questions on the application form. He paid the due and was a member.

"Go to the room at the end of the hall and put all your clothes in any empty locker," the lady at the disk advised.

"Huh?" Poor Pete questioned.

"Take off your clothes and join those people at the beach." This was more like a command. Poor Pete complied. Leaving the security of the building, Poor Pete naked, and feeling vulnerable and insecure, took a faltering step. Nakedness did not boost his self confidence. He could not go directly to the group on the beach. His hesitant footsteps led him on a tangent. Then he paused, looking down at his bare feet he spied a bit of metal. Retrieving it, it proved to be a Chevy Emblem with a key on a short chain.

Glancing up from his find, he saw the one-girl welcoming committee coming to him in a bee line. One quick look was all he could muster courage for. She had dark, shoulder length hair and a perfect body with a golden tan. All she had on was the tan and a smile. Poor Pete couldn't look.

In a rich feminine voice she said, "Good Morning, you must be a new member."

Poor Pete glanced at her well-shaped ankle but couldn't bring his eyes to look a bit higher. He tried to answer but his Adams Apple had turned sideways on him.

Holding out a hand, she invited, "Don't feel strange. Come and join our gang." Poor Pete had never held a girl's hand who was fully dressed, let alone one that was fully undressed.

This time he glanced as high as her shapely knee. His Adams Apple turned the rest of the way around. His face was red. He was about to choke. In utter misery he turned to the left, regained the building, put on his clothes and went home.

The question that Poor Pete pondered the rest of his days was, "How on earth could a person lose a Chevy key at a nudist camp?"

The End of the Devil

Viola and Catherine were Uncle Charlie and Aunt Gerty's girls. They were only little tykes that week in July when the Nuns from Gravelbourg came to Hodgeville to teach catechism classes for a couple of weeks. On the hot tiresome afternoon of the first day, the good Sisters described the bad situation in the Garden of Eden. There was Adam, Eve, the apple, the devil and the snake all mixed up in one scary story. The little people squirmed and sweated through the lesson.

Adult evaluation saved the girls from more classes. They should possibly wait one year and then resume religious studies. The bad deal was that Eden was all they had to go on for that year.

After the thrashing crew left, and there was the big new straw pile out past the barn, Aunt Gerty had to go to Gravelbourg to get some dental work done. It would be quite likely that their Mom and Dad would not be home before the kids got home from school. Therefore, rules were laid out. When you get home, change into play clothes and hang up your school clothes. If you go out to play, stay away from the new straw pile. It has not settled yet and could slide down and bury you, so do not go near it. Be good girls until we get home.

The walk home from school was shared part way with neighbour children. The danger of the straw pile was discussed at long length and with much wisdom by this gang of five people (whose total combined age would not reach thirty.) It was brought out that a calf had died in a straw slide, and that had happened past Uncle Joe's lake.

Parting with their friends, they trudged home. The rules were followed, clothes changed and hung up, and out to play. The forbidden straw pile was huge and yellow and quiet looking. To get a better view, Vi and Catherine had to crawl under the gate to the barn yard. Catherine had a small two-foot part of a tree branch in her hand. At the granary where the wheat had been thrashed into, the girls wondered at the massive pile of straw.

One of the girls screamed, "Look over in the weeds, there is a black and yellow snake." Catherine was armed. She went on the offensive. Vi grabbed a stick lying by the building and joined the battle.

The snake was trying so hard to get home free in the new straw pile, but he didn't make it. Poor Mr. Garter Snake lay there, his little body beaten to a pulp and devoid of life.

The girls were elated beyond their wildest dreams. They had possibly attained a level of blessedness for mankind, unknown since the episode at Eden. Still carrying their weapons, the heroines crawled under the gate, and glowing with accomplishment made their way to the house. The return of their parents was the crown of roses for their good fortune.

Before Uncle Charlie was out of the car, there were his daughters jumping up and down shouting with joy, "Daddy, Daddy, WE JUST KILLED THE DEVIL!"

Now, a statement that great had to be investigated. The little girls led their father out to the new straw pile where he could see for himself the remains of the snake. They didn't get much credit for the snake but caught a bit of the devil for being too close to the new straw pile. Luckily, it was Catherine's little switch that Uncle Charlie used sparingly on the bottoms of his two little girls, just to make sure rules were rules and adhered to.

Driving Lessons

"Lady, do you really give driving lessons?" This was a personal little joke among the four of us. On an evening when we were together and Berniece made a move like spilling a card when she shuffled the deck, "Say, lady, do you give driving lessons?" Or if Joanne dropped a spoon in the kitchen, "Lady, do you need driving lessons?"

Jim was serving in the Canadian Army in Holland where he met Joanne, a tall, slim beautiful, blonde Dutch girl. She came to Canada as a war bride. When we got to know them, they already had two small boys.

One day Jim asked me, "Do you think that Berniece could help Joanne get acquainted with the Pontiac? You know, ride around with her and give her some pointers."

"I'll talk it over with her tonight and we'll give you a call."

Jim Edwards and I both wore white combination overalls with MID WEST MOTORS in blue letters across the back. Jim knew exactly what kind of a car he wanted. When it turned up on the used car lot, he snapped up the deal. To us in the trade it was 51-27-69 which meant that it was a 1951 model, four door sedan, American built Pontiac. The 27 stood for 'deluxe'. With all the extra chrome mouldings that decorated the sides of the car, it would take an extra hour to wash and polish it.

It was all arranged for the next day. Berniece would come to the garage with me after lunch and take the Edward's car back to Joanne. They would drive around for the afternoon. After work, I was to drive Jim home and we would all have supper at their house.

When Berniece was at the Edward's front door, little Joey, the four-year-old neighbour looked up with big round eyes and with honest wonder asked, "Lady, do you really give driving lessons?" My wife laughed and said, "Not really, we are just going for a drive."

It was a smooth ride around the city. Stop signs, traffic lights, and uncontrolled intersections were no problem to Joanne. It was such a nice day that they extended the trip. They left Regina and went west on a dirt road. The plan was to go ten miles out and return. They would park the car and have a cup of tea. Joanne drove very well until they got to the long new grade. The construction had been done the summer before and the edges had not settled, the dirt was still soft and loose. Mrs. Edwards got slightly off the hard packed track, the Pontiac veered to the left. For the next hundred yards the new ruts in the soft dirt were straight, even and angling at a precarious slant on the side of the grade, determined to reach the water.

"Joanne! Turn left. GET DOWN IN THE DITCH!"

In a tea party voice she answered, "No, I don't want to go in the ditch. I want to get back on the road." With that she cramped the wheels to the right. This just helped to cut a wider trench in the side of the road and to pile up more dirt on the lower side of the car, which possibly prevented it from rolling over.

"Joanne, I think you better stop."

"Should I back up to get on the road?"

"NO! Just stop."

The brakes were applied, ignition turned off, and all was quiet.

"Joanne, let's go out this door. It will be closer to climb to the top of the road." The door on the high side of the car would not open very far because of the loose dirt in the way. They made their exit and Berniece closed the door very softly. Their tracks up the side of the grade were more than ankle deep. All this and no panic, but as they looked down on the roof of the car, the ladies did become perturbed.

Guardian Angels run in packs. One kept the car from rolling over. Another guided a farmer with a John Deere along the road. Stopping his tractor, he had a look at the situation "Not many people drive on that part of the road." The third and fourth angels helped him get the car back on the road without the ladies getting involved.

Jim was somewhat upset when he was shown the site. Joanne's next driving was in Calgary where she took drivers' training.

Three decades later we had matching grey hair. Urban life and the capital city were long in the past. We were raising cattle near the far edge of the parkland of Saskatchewan and I got stuck in the muskeg. As I walked away, I looked back. The Case tractor was a faded cream color. The way it sat in the mud it was the shape and color of a lazy pig that would rise up in front but sit on its hind legs. The rear wheels were down deep. The front wheels were still on top which was in my favor. Where would you hitch onto a New Holland bale wagon to pull it backwards without tearing it apart? I didn't find an answer to that problem, so it would have to be pulled forward. What I had to do was walk home, start the four wheel drive Versatile tractor and get the cable and chains stashed away behind the seat in the cab. I would have to drive the machine near the house and go in and ask my partner to come and drive one of the tractors.

My partner was baking cookies. That was not too hard to accept. While the last pan was in the oven, I was able to taste-test the first batch.

We maneuvered the four wheel to a little rise at the edge of the swampy hay meadow. I left the diesel running at a slow idle and strung out the cable and chain, all one hundred and seventy feet of it. With the chain hooked securely to the Case tractor, I started its engine and gave the signal for forward. The big tractor started to move and the cable and chain became tight. The rear wheels of the bogged down Case tractor started to rise, then dropped back. She had stalled the motor.

She opened the door of the Versatile and called with a little Joey voice, "Say Mister, do you give driving lessons?"

Home Improvements

Canadian Sawmills of Prince George, British Columbia was located thirty miles south of the city, near Stone Creek. The camp was one half mile from the highway, right beside the creek. The timbered ridge on the south side of the creek was so high that, in December and January, we couldn't see the sun at high noon. The rise on the other side was just as high but not as steep. A winding trail led a half mile up the hill to the mill.

On a cool, quite, Sunday afternoon, Woodrow and I went up to the mill and beyond. He had spotted a Birch tree that was five inches across, and clear of branches for seven feet. He marked it on the south side, and cut it down. I had to go farther into the forest before a similar tree was found. Marking it on what I considered was the south side, I cut it down. It was a long old tramp to the mill with that log on my shoulder.

On Monday, Sulo, the edgerman, had our Birch cut into two-by-fours. From there it was lighter and down hill to carry them to our bunk house. After a few weeks the wood had dried enough to tell if it would (or would not) make skis.

Woodrow's were perfect. On a level surface all four corners would touch even, at the center of the board the arch was nearly two inches, just right for skis. Mine were not so good. They ended up being warped.

"So, you want to make airplane propellers?" Sulo asked me. "You did not get the mark on the south side."

"No. The sun was behind the cloud so I had to guess."

Sulo had skied in Finland when he was a kid. He also learned how to make skis. This was the art that he was going to pass on to us. I watched Woodrow make his skis.

On a sunny Sunday, I went to mark my Birch at high noon. I thought it was a long distance to carry my first log, but that was nothing compared to the trip I had to make for the next ski wood. It was close to a mile above the mill where I found two trees that were just right. The second one was a spare, just in case one or the other would warp. I was

146

tired by the time I had the two logs at the mill. In time it was proven that I had two top quality sets of ski material. By the time my wood was dry enough to carve, it was spring breakup, and time to go home. George, the lumber trucker, took my bundle of Birch into town for me. It was shipped express collect to Hodgeville, Saskatchewan. The express bill cost me six dollars and forty cents. We had worked for eight dollars a day less one dollar for room and board. The shipment of wood left me sixty cents of one days work.

Uncle Reinhardt had his truck in town so he took the boards home and stored them. Fifteen years later I returned to the farm and went to get my precious Birch.

"I just had to have a piece of hard wood at harvest time, so I cut two feet off one of your boards. Will that matter?" asked my uncle.

"No, you can keep the pair of boards," I replied. The remaining two boards were put in the basement at home for secure keeping.

Still later, my wife Berniece was hosting a barbecue. A recurring problem raised its ugly head. With only two people at the picnic table and on the same side, it would tip over. Grandpa Doll had the answer,

"If I could get two two-by-four boards, and nail one on each end, it would fix the problem."

"I know. There are two in the basement," said the lady of the house.

When I came from the field and stopped the John Deere, I saw grandpa working at the picnic table. As I drew near, he straightened up, laid the hand saw on the table and mopped his brow.

"Look at that. This sure is hard wood, but I got some of the nails in," he declared, pointing to the bottom of the legs at the far end of the table. There was six feet, or three quarters of one of my ski boards, nailed to the table leg. Grandpa pointed to the other board, "Its darn tough wood, but I have this one half cut. I'll get it yet."

My ski wood! Carried for miles on my shoulder, cost most of a days wages, aged for twenty years, and made into legs for the picnic table. I...well...well, my goodness.

147

Meat in the Pot

It was the middle of March. The sun was streaming in the window. Leo and I were remembering other springs. It was late March and he had the Whitefish brothers helping with fences and rocks and those things that have to be done before working on the land. The brothers lived in their tent near the cows. Leo continued to tell the following story.

"Two o'clock one morning, Andrew Whitefish came to the house. "Leo! Come quick! It might be a bear in with the cows. They are making lots of noise. I never hear like dat before."

I grabbed my 30.06 Winchester and followed him back to the small barb wire fenced pasture where we had the cows. It was fairly dark, and I couldn't see anything wrong so I stood still and waited. The cows had settled down quite a bit. I moved to the corner of the fence and stood there. In time there was a break in the clouds so we got some moonlight. Just then there was a big commotion at the edge of the herd. An animal came out of the willows by the creek, walked past the cows and was coming in my direction but, a ways to my right. This thing was ambling along on all four feet. Soon the fence wire squeaked, the sun of a gun went right through it.

It was not moving fast, and I got a good broadside shot. The thing flopped over and put out a terrifying squeal. The men came running with a flashlight. Yes sir, there it was, a six hundred-pound muddy, boar pig, deader than a mackerel.

I said, "Dress it out fellas. You might as well use the meat." Then I went back to bed.

The weather stayed nice and things went along good. Later, Mike came shuffling into the yard with four days of whiskers on his cheeks, tears in his eyes, and the breeze fluttering his frayed overalls.

"Have you seen a big boar at your place? Mine got away and I've been looking for him for three days," Mike said and gave me a hopeful squint.

"What colour is he?"

"He's white, but he's got a black scabby spot on his neck."

"I suppose you need him home for breeding."

"No, I'm finished with him but I don't want to lose him. He is a big one."

"Where did you get him?"

"At the Saskatoon Auction Mart. I paid sixty bucks for him, and now I got to haul him back there."

"Well, I tell you Mike, your pig was over here bothering the cows the night before last and I shot him."

Mike scuffed his toe around in the dirt for a few seconds and looked a little bit sad. The tears nearly returned.

"Mike would you take sixty bucks for your pig now?"

"Sure. Yes. Uh ha, that would be good."

I got out my wallet and handed Mike three twenties. He thanked me, "Thank you, thanks. Thanks," and went home.

Everybody was happy except the Indians. I asked how the meat was?

"Can't cook it. Smells so strong, keeps blowing the lid off the pot.""

The Road North

"If I was 19 years old again, I would not hesitate a minute to do that job again," said Grandpa Doll. We were sitting in the house, smelling the 1982 Christmas turkey that we would soon attack. Grandma and Grandpa were spending Christmas with our family at the Spruce Creek Ranch.

"It was at the end of June 1919 when George Muri, Bill Innis and I started north to Loon Lake, Saskatchewan with thirty-two of Ben Newton's Percheron mares. Each one of us was nineteen years old. George and Bill were to ride and take care of the stock. I drove the chuck wagon and did the cooking. We had an eight by sixteen-foot tent stretched over a hay rack, just a perfect fit. We had hay and grain for the horses, our bedrolls, a stove, table and food, all under canvas.

I had a good team on the wagon. When they turned the herd out of the corral, those horses just ran. I had to drive hard to keep them in sight. I got to the south slope of Wiwa Creek and there were the horses, going over the north slope and out of sight again. Ben had told us where to stop for the night so I slowed down, no use killing the team the first day.

When I got to the southeast edge of Swift Current, it was no trouble to see the path taken by thirty-two horses as they went west along South Railway Street. After they crossed the bridge, there was no more manure on the street, only horse tracks in the Chinese Market Gardens. Later the guys told me they had been attacked by hoes shovels and weed cutters.

The camp, in a coulee north of the city, was a good one for the first day. We had to push right along to get to The Landing on the next day. Our orders were to ferry the wagon, and swim the herd across the South Saskatchewan River. An hour before we got to the river, the ferry cable broke and the ferry went eight miles downstream. There was a lad with a horse and buggy loaded with crates of eggs on the craft. The ferry operator managed to get lodged near the south bank of the river. He and his passenger had nothing but raw eggs to live on until they got rescued the next day.

They had eight big work horses hitched four and four ahead on a long cable that was tied to the ferry. By using the rudder on the ferry they kept it out in water deep enough to float it. With the horse power they were able to tow the boat back to the Landing in a day. A couple more days and they had the ferry going. We had to herd the horses on the river flat for those few days. It was no use getting the herd across without the chuck wagon. If I had tried to swim the wagon across the river, it would have ended up floating past Saskatoon later in the summer.

To buy a loaf of bread was sometimes hard to do. One of the guys would ride to a farmhouse and ask, sometimes we'd get three loaves, sometimes none. We had hoped to use railroad stock yards for night holding, but that hardly ever happened.

There had been some heavy rains out to the north west of us. Somewhere in the Biggar area, the trail crossed a shallow creek. I could tell that the mares had crossed there between the willows. It looked deep but I had no choice, so in we went. It was only a hundred feet across but I was only sixty feet out when the back end of the rack floated off of the back wagon bolster. I got the team out of the water but the wagon had to stay in. If I had pulled it out it would have tipped over. I tied the horses to the willows and crawled into the wagon and had a snooze. When the guys got hungry they would come back looking for me.

George put his lariat on the rack and used his horse to pull it sideways while Bill and I lifted, that way we got it loaded again. By the time we got up to where the horses were grazing and got supper eaten, it was past bed time.

It was ordinary travelling until we got to Battleford. We pulled in there in the early forenoon. The RCMP stopped us. For the rest of the day we herded the stock where the industrial part of town is, west of the number four and south of the number sixteen highways. The law did not want us to interfere with day time traffic crossing the river. At 2:00 A.M. we got word to move. There was a Mountie at the north end of the bridge stopping anyone going south. Another rode with George, just ahead of the horse herd. There was the third cop riding with Bill behind the herd. Behind me and the wagon, were two more Mounted Police. They led us right through the main drag of North Battleford. Out north of the city they said "Well boys, good bye and good luck." It was four o'clock then, and daylight, so we kept travelling on.

It was between Turtleford and Loon Lake that we were on a narrow trail through the aspen forest. We had just finished our noon meal when a brown face, with a black hat and braids, poked his head in. "Grub?" was all he said. I fixed him a big plate of food. He swallowed it down and went on his way.

George took Bill's .32 Ivor Johnson revolver, the one we had been counting on for the ultimate protection once we got in Indian country. He emptied the shells out, took it by the end of the barrel and flung it as far as he could into the bush.

"There, now maybe we'll be safe," was all he said.

Dance Class

On the first Saturday in July, I rode along with Basil to the tap dance class that was being organized at the Coughlin farm. Mom said 'no' to my being a pupil. The tuition was small, but so was the cash income that year. Doris Myers, a lovely young lady who lived with her brothers, sister, and father Lou on their farm near Vanguard, was the teacher.

At the farmhouse, the fathers, George, Fred and Lou, sat on chairs and a box in the porch. I sat on the step with Gilman. I suppose, knowing that I was there, caused him to do something that got him expelled from the class. That's why he joined me on the step. The fathers had not mentioned the drought. It had been with us for a few years, so it had been well talked out long ago. All they said was, "It sure is hot."

A soft breeze rolled a big round gray Russian Thistle in the driveway. It stopped midway between the house and the barn. It may have come clear across the Campbell section to the west of Coughlins, but there it lazed in the heat and sunshine. In the distance we could hear Doris' voice and occasionally a note of the piano. The gentlemen made some mention of some election. That had no interest for Gilman and I.

Lou went on to tell, "When I worked in the livery stable, the sheriff came along one day and asked if I was old enough to vote? I told him, 'Sure. I just turned twenty-one.' This fat guy eased up beside me, and with a slick hand motion, put a five-dollar bill in my pocket. 'Just remember me when you get in the polling booth.' This sheriff had gotten very fat and lazy on the job and he sure wanted to keep it.

I watched him really close for the next three weeks. I must have seen him do that slick hand trick with the five-dollar bill more than twenty times. The poor old guy just could not understand why, after giving away all those fivers, that he only got four votes." Lou finished his story. Gilman and I found the story very amusing. The fathers remarked on the legality, the dishonour, the stupidity and every other angle of the case.

153

"Oh, I kept the five dollars, but I was too smart to vote for him," Lou explained.

The wind came up a bit, the thistle rolled into the coulee. The dance class was dismissed. We all went home.

The following Saturday I stayed home. Gilman was reinstated in the class.

Language Lesson

When we moved to the Spruce Creek ranch, between the Pelican Band Reserve and the Forest Reserve, I took a soft-footed approach to our Cree neighbours. One afternoon in town, I was met by Wooden Leg Jim, Jim Lewis was his real name.

"Say, I'd like a ride home to my place," he said.

"Climb in. I go right past there."

Before we went by the airport, Jim offered me a cigarette. I shoved it in my mouth and kept right on driving. He turned to me and said, "MIGGETS" (or some thing that sounded like that). All I could do was to return a blank stare.

"Don't you know nothing?" was Jim's question.

"What are you talking about?" was my question.

"Miggets. We need a match to light these things." I fished in my pocket, found a book of matches and soon we were soaking in the nicotine.

"Can't you talk any Cree?" he asked.

"Heck no, Jim. You are about the only Cree I have ever talked to."

"Danzy Zeine."

"What does that mean?" I asked.

"I said Greetings, or Hello, or How are you today?".

I pondered this for a bit. All that in two words.

"In English it would be, `Is your sun shining today?' It don't have to be the sun in sky. You got big trouble, it not matter how bright the sky, you got no sunshine."

Jim's house came too soon for a complete lesson in Cree language and psychology.

A week later, on a dark night, two Indian ladies drove into the ranch yard. I answered a gentle rap on the door. The younger person asked, "Want to buy some fresh fish?"

"I want to see them first." I said.

155

The fish were in an old wash tub in the back of the Ford truck. It was a black truck and so was the night.

"You got flashlight?" was her next question.

"No, batteries dead," I answered. That started a brief discussion in Cree between the ladies. Miggets was the only word that I got out of the conversation. With more reflex than gallant intelligence, I handed the older person a book of paper matches.

With a look, rather than a word, my offer was disdainfully declined. She unbuttoned her beaded jacket, reached for a wooden match in her sweater pocket, buttoned up the jacket, and struck the match. The breeze blew it out. She said a word that sounded like, "Ahhhh sit."

This gal wore a new buckskin coat. The button holes were tight and troublesome. In all good time another match was struck. The head broke off of this one. There was that word again, "Ahhhhhh sit."

The third match was brought out with the same routine. Unbutton, fish out the match, do up the tight buttonholes, strike the match, and it blew out. There it was again, "Ahhhhhh sit."

"What is she saying?" I asked the young lady.

Her answer was, "What is the matter with you? She is talking English."

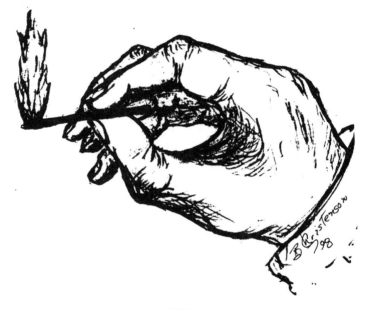

Water Holes

The importance of water holes cannot be over stressed. With Canada on the north, the Mississippi to the east, the Rio Grande on the south and the Rocky Mountains on the west, these rivers and rocks form the boundary of the western plains. The first people to rush into the vacuum left by the departing buffalo were the stockmen with herds of cattle. Nutritious rich grass, waving knee-high in the breeze was a dream come true to the newcomers.

The rivers in this new land ran from west to east, and were not very close together. A cow cannot walk many miles for a drink of water without upsetting her energy balance. In the hot summer months the ranchers had to depend on small lakes or springs for water for their livestock.

One of the aggravations of these early settlers was the culprit that would homestead a water hole. He would build a sturdy fence around the water hole to deprive the animals of a drink. That made the surrounding grass useless.

For an exorbitant amount of money, this person would sell his property and go in search of another water hole.

At the height of the depression of the 1930's, a group of large American Corporations opened branch plants in Southern Ireland. These people, like the cattlemen of the early west, were trying to improve their profit picture.

A young Irishman applied to his government for the trademarks of these companies and had them registered in his name. It was perfectly legal at the time.

When the American companies were set up and ready to produce, they found that they had to buy their trademarks from the new owner. He netted about seven million bucks.

The son of a gun just homesteaded the water holes.

157

Hotel

The old three story building was coming down, board by board. It was built in the heady year of 1912. When the thing was completed, it sported a sign that called it the Vanguard Hotel. The hotel could boast a rotunda with an L shaped oak registration desk and a spacious dining room. There was a huge range that devoured shovels of coal and was the heart of the kitchen. There was a coal fired boiler in the basement that provided steam heat to every room. It was a grand place for the up and coming boom town of Vanguard.

Farm folks sometimes spent the night, travelling business people called it home for a night, anyone needing food and shelter, found it at the hotel. There were no drinks served but a few party type guys, would rent a room and bring their own booze.

Charlie was older than my parents. He related this tale to me when I was in my teens.

"One night I saw the doctor jump start a guy's heart and he didn't even have jumper cables. There was Harry, Joe, Bill, Hank, Jim and I having a few drinks one Saturday night. You know Harry and Hank. Joe and Bill went back east years ago. There were six of us having an inebriated social evening in the far southeast corner room of the third floor.

These partly refined gentlemen were a bit noisy, but not so much that they were a bother to any other guest of the hotel. This room was very close to the stairway leading downstairs, which happened to be lucky for the revellers. It was well after midnight and the party was rolling right along.

Jim, sitting on the edge of the bed gave a gasp and shudder. Without further ado, he flopped on the bed, his mouth open and breathless, his eyes open but sightless. Someone said, "Jim's dead." Two of the guys tried to wake Jim up.

Jim was deader'n a door nail. The fourth one went down the stairs, three steps at a time. The local doctor occupied the room beside the stairway on the second floor.

Pounding on the doctor's door he shouted, "Doc, come quick! I think Jim might be dead." The messenger and doctor went up the stairs nearly as fast as the former had come down. Reaching the patient, the doctor made a fast check of an eye ball, then his neck for a pulse, There was none!

"Quick give me whiskey." The doctor called.

As Charlie told it many years later, "I had the last half a bottle in my hands. "NO! Doc, NO! It was whiskey that killed him." Well, I figured I was thinking much clearer than Doc so, I got backed in the corner and held onto the bottle for dear life. The doctor's reflexes were better than mine so he got the bottle away from me.

They got Jim's body in a sitting position with a guy holding each shoulder, while the Doc dribbled whiskey in his mouth and massaged his throat.

A few seconds of that and the doctor said, "Hold him up now." The doctor doubled up his fist, took aim at Jim's brisket bone. He hit him as hard as he could. Jim gave one mighty gasp for air, focussed his eyes and started breathing.

The doctor said, "Whiskey is bad for people." He took our bottle and went back to bed."

"What happened to Jim?"

Charlie's careless answer surprised me, "Oh he went to B.C. about thirty-five years ago. He died a couple of years ago. He must have had some kind of heart trouble."

Science With Luck

The sporting type men and boys considered Abner an all around good guy. The women of the community thought that he spent too much time in the beer parlour or fishing. It was the ladies reasoning, "He always has three days growth of that gray beard on, so what would his bachelor shack look like?"

Abner spoke. "Well seeing as I am the oldest one sitting around this here campfire, and have the information first hand, I can tell you guys the straight facts.

It was the French that got the first heat aimed missile going, and it was a fishing trip just like this one we are on that finally gave 'em the big breakthrough and success. This Perrier Roabadoo, or something like that, had worked in his lab for years trying to work up a system that would guide a missile to a hot jet plane. This Perrier fella had been with the French in Viet Nam when they had to pack up their tents and high-tail it home. I think it was in '54. Now, Roaby had this idea that if you could point a missile up in the air, fire it and have it find its own way to the enemy plane and blow it up, you would never have to pack up and go home till you were good and ready.

He tried thermal triggers, then micro chip boards, acid mixes, even an oxygen hydrogen borozino combination. Each one of these took considerable time to get made. The test on the last one code named OHB darn near scuttled the project. Roaby test fired it the same day the President was going to the sea shore for a few days of rest. The Pres' limo had just turned a tight curve on the mountain road when there was a tremendous blast behind the car. Part of the mountain was turned into instant gravel.

The President and body guards knew for sure it was the work of middle east terrorists. The Pres was so shook up that he stayed an extra three weeks at the beach, setting in a lounge chair and wearing the largest, darkest, sunglasses you ever saw. You can just imagine that he enjoyed the scenery through those big blue-green lenses.

Roaby's missile had followed the center line in the highway but it had too much speed to make the curve, or it would have been lights out with the Pres and his limo. The poor man of science went home feeling pretty low. His wife told him he should go to Canada and see if he could find any relatives and get his mind off that stupid missile.

In Montreal he drew a blank. He had no luck in Toronto either. At Winnipeg things took a turn for the better when the records of a long ago marriage came to light. Roaby's great great uncle met a Nell MacGregor. Well soon they were going around like two pups in the moonlight. Mr. MacGregor would not have his Nell marry a Roabadoo, so great great uncle changed his name to MacTavish, married the girl and went to live in Saskatchewan.

When Roaby got to Saskatchewan and found Marcel MacTavish, his distant cousin, they hit it off real good. After a few days of visiting they went down to the small lake behind Marcel's to try their luck at fishing. The fish weren't biting but the mosquitoes were. The cousin from France had never seen anything like Marcel's flying insects.

All night long he tossed and turned, and by morning the idea had set root. He would examine the aimers of the mosquitoes from the lake if he could only get them home to the lab. Cousin Marcel explained to the scientist that only the female mosquitoes bite. They need the protein from red blood to develop eggs.

The men put cheese cloth over the ends of a calendar tube and filled it with Marcel's mosquitoes. They also put a bit of tomato juice in the tube as a pacifier for the trip. Roaby flew back to his lab in Paris. Well sir, it wasn't too long until Roaby had the mosquito heat sensing component grafted into his missile.

The government came up with some old derelict planes and some Non Com fliers that didn't handle their drinks well, and used them for missile testers. The first three planes came down all right. They were each hit at the base of a wing. It took a lot of detective work to see through that one.

After a while Roaby learned that he had been using the armpit biting type mosquito. So, it took another load of Marcel's bugs from the little lake, and a lot more research and it was still a matter of chance as to where the darn missile would go. The lab had this test beach in the basement where they did all sorts of outside and sea shore experiments. By now there was a big crew working on the secret missile project. They had the cute steno, Gergette, sit in her bikini on the fake beach all day long to attract and test the Saskatchewan mosquitoes.

The loss of insects was staggering. It was a big job to get the test beach so the study material could not fly away. The ankle and wrist biters were discarded right away. There were a fair number of back and arm pit biters recovered, but something was missing. They were still losing mosquitoes like crazy. It was on the seventh load that Marcel shipped over, that Roaby found out that Gergette was swattin' those that landed on her tummy, just slapping them into flat smudges with her bare hands. That is just human reaction to pesky mosquitoes.

When that little problem was straightened out it wasn't long till Roaby was on the road to developing the aimers for the back and belly striking weapons. With the brains or homing device of the Saskatchewan mosquitoes sorted and installed, the French Military had three grades of missiles. The Arm Pit, it was effective but only took one wing off the target plane. The Fisherman, it only struck in the back, it was deadly. The one named after the pretty research girl Gergette, aimed for the belly of the target and it was pure dynamite.

When word leaked out about this new missile, the whole world's military went into a tailspin. Canada put a halt to exporting mosquitoes to anyplace, but by then Marcel had made enough money from the mosquito sales to the French Military that he was able to buy a Cessna and open his own fly-in fishing camp.

Yes sirree, that's just the way Marcel MacTavish told me the whole thing. Did someone spray inside the tent for mosquitoes?"

The Lost Art

Ott's hi-jinks had been going on for two years longer than Saskatchewan politics. He came with his parents to the Assiniboia Territory to locate near the Cypress Hills. Time and place dictated that this fellow become a cowboy.

His training took place at the time of open ranges, wild cattle, and partly civilized horses. For a while he rode, stirrup to stirrup, with a bronze mustached ex cavalry officer from Virginia. "That man rode erect and proud in his flat army saddle," Ott remembered, "He was the Boss."

Cowboys are cowboys, but it is not written in stone that they had to keep at it. Ott was intrigued by the blacksmith, welding two pieces of iron together, a hammer, forge and some gray powder, was all it took. Our friend tried this trade. This led to Spokane, Washington where he became a machinist. Never one to say whoa, he turned to auto ignition and carburetion.

When I got to know Ott, he was more than seventy years old. White hair, keen blue eyes behind steel rimed glasses. He was tall and slim. His face was smooth with sharp features. His mind was sharp too. Ott was a tune-up man at the Buick dealership where we both worked.

One Monday morning in March, Ott and I were the first two in the coffee room.

"Say, I haven't seen Clem around today," I remarked.

Ott took a small sip from his mug and said, "I suppose he would be in jail if they could find him." He set his coffee cup down to explain, "Clem was having a really wild time Saturday night. Sometime early yesterday morning he went tearing down 5th Avenue North. He just crossed the bridge where he rolled his convertible. It lay on its side right by the creek until the cops had it towed away. Clem had become very scarce.

When I drove by, there was a bunch of people standing by the edge of the creek. There, right out on the ice, about twenty feet away, was a jug of wine, three quarters full. Between the shore and the jug was ten feet of open water. On the other side it was about the same, honeycombed ice. Boy, that jug sure looked good. Red wine sparkling in the sunlight. We figured that it was chilled just right too."

Another sip of coffee then he added, "Late in the afternoon it melted through the ice. A dead loss."

"Well why didn't an old cowboy like you get a lariat and flip over it, if it was that close?" I questioned.

Ott had a wistful look, "You know, it's too bad, sometimes old cowboys don't remember just how smart they used to be."

Fearsome Trip

It was near the end of March. What little snow we had, had been gone for weeks. It was warm that morning. In fact, before I left Swift Current, I took my jacket off and threw it on the truck seat. I was wheeling north on number 4 highway. I hoped that I would get the hay loaded at Duck Lake and be home before dark.

It was a mile north of Kyle that I saw him, a bent old man. A long brown overcoat hung from his wide shoulders. He walked stooped because of the heavy suit case in one hand and a large twine-tied cardboard box in the other. With a hint of human kindness, I stopped to offer the poor pilgrim a ride. When I reached over to open the door, there he was with his head about even with the bottom of the door. And what a face! Wrinkled, bearded, and a disturbing stare.

"Where are you headed for?" I asked.

"I'm going to Delisle," he answered.

"I'm going right through there, climb in," I invited. I was not impressed by his looks. An old cloth cap covered a rim of white hair. However, I did not think that looks alone should condemn a man to walk a hundred miles on a day like this. He wanted to put his luggage in the box, but I said, "No, it would be too hard to get it out. Put your suitcase on the seat between us. The box will fit on the floor."

I reasoned that if he was not just mentally right, he would not have much room to manoeuver about.

Just a day or two before that, there was a gruesome bit on a news cast about a hitch hiker shooting a kindly motorist. He got the door shut and we wheeled on north. A few miles farther, he unbuttoned his coat, and squirmed his arms out of the sleeves. Under his coat he wore a heavy wool jacket. It was the kind of jacket you might find in a western wear store. Out of the corner of my eye I saw him give me a beady look and reach furtively under his jacket to his left arm pit. My goodness! There was a big bulge right there. Could he have a shoulder holster, or just a hand gun somehow in his shirt pocket? He withdrew his hand, and sat quit calm.

Some minutes elapsed and he repeated the act, complete with that scary squint. This move put me a wee bit on edge, but he did not pull his gun. No, not yet. It sure did look like a hand gun under his jacket. An attack would call for a counterattack. I settled on my plan. The ditches beside the road were well sloped and dry. If he drew a gun, I would drive across the ditch then back across the road, then across to the other ditch. I might roll my truck, but if I was to be shot, would the truck matter?

Beyond Rosetown the ditches were not so inviting, but by now he was just patting that bulge. "It's time to come down to earth! Relax, start with my head, then neck, shoulders, arms, and on through the rest of my body," I silently told myself. Then the son of a gun gave me another dirty look. Well, "What the heck?" I thought. I may as well keep on relaxing.

When we got to Delisle, I stopped to phone Mr. Gardner at Duck Lake to let him know when I would be at the haystack. Leaving the pay phone, I went back across the street to the truck. He was still sitting there.

"Where would you like to stop?" I asked.

"Up at the service station where they have the café," was the reply.

We stopped at the designated spot. He said, "Come in, I want to buy you a steak."

"No, thank you." I replied.

"At least come in for a coffee," he sort of pleaded.

"Sorry, I have to hurry. I wouldn't want to keep Mr. Gardner waiting at the stack yard. It's twelve miles out of town."

Then he reached inside his jacket and brought out the bulge. "How much do I owe you for the ride?" he asked. In his hand he held his wallet. It was so stuffed with bills that it could not fold. If it only contained one dollar bills he was not hard up. In his shirt pocket that wallet would take up the same space as a small six gun.

"Not a cent old timer. I'm glad that you got here okay and good luck to you," was my feeble reply. Imagine that! The old guy had been afraid that I would steal his money.

The Feeling

"It was during the second world war. You couldn't buy repair parts. There were a lot of things that you couldn't buy." That was how Andy remembered those times. He then related the following story.

I was running the service station over on Third Avenue. Ed, a doctor of Entomology, drove in with a government car from the Experimental Farm. He darn near ran into the side of the building. His brakes were completely shot. He wanted them fixed.

I asked him if he had any parts.

He said, "No, the government employees can't get repair parts either, at least not soon enough. I've got to get this car fixed now."

So I got his car in, and got underneath. I was having quite a struggle. After awhile the doctor asked if I wanted a drink. Well it was blazing hot, so I said, "Sure." He handed me a Coke. It was mixed kind of strong, but the break job sort of fell into place. We road tested the car. It worked real good.

The doctor asked if I wanted another shot. I said, "Of course."

He said, "Get a Coke and spill out about an inch."

I handed him my empty Coke bottle and told him that I'd just have it straight.

He asked, "Are you sure about that?"

"Yup, I'm sure." I told him.

He poured less than a half inch in my bottle. I tossed it down. For twenty seconds I was turned to stone. I couldn't breathe. I couldn't cough. I couldn't blink. When I got my voice back, I asked, "What under the sun was that?" The doctor laughed, "That is what we use in the lab to pickle bugs."

Andy finished the story by saying, "That's how I know what a pickled bug feels like."

That reminded me of another story I had heard: At one time in Alberta, you couldn't buy anything that had alcohol in it. They made big vats of beer, here at the brewery, and shipped it to other provinces. It had

167

been a hot day in July and it was a thirsty kind of night. Well, these two coal miners found out the number on a box car that was loaded with beer kegs.

These guys took a chalk, tape measure, a bit and brace, a wash tub and two tin cups. When they found the right box car in the Canadian Pacific freight yard, they crawled under and measured from the side and end. Then they put a chalk mark underneath a number of kegs. The plan was to drill through the floor of the car and into a keg. Hole after hole they drilled into thin air. By now it was getting late. They thought maybe they were given the wrong car number. The width of the boxcar wall had not been considered. That was why they drilled all the holes between the kegs. Before they gave up, one guy moved over and drilled a hole without a mark. HOORAY! He hit beer.

In the morning the railroad security people found the two guys sleeping beside the tub of beer. They were sent off to jail. I know how they felt when they were looking for the boxcar, but after that I don't know how they felt. I have never been in jail.

A Friend

"Sam passed away last night," Norman informed me.

"Oh, that's too bad," I responded.

"The funeral will be on Thursday," he said.

"Will you be going to it?" I wondered.

"I sure am," was Norman's answer. "You'll have to run the place alone. I won't be in at all that day."

I thought that Sam and Norman were good friends. I understood better when Norman told me how it came about.

After school, Norman had a half mile walk down the hill and across the bridge, a ways farther he would be home. On one afternoon, he got home as usual and asked for something to eat. His mom gave him a half an apple. His dad had a big surprise.

"Boy, you should see what we have in the garage." The six-year-old, munching on the apple, wandered off in the direction of the garage. Along the way he picked up a rust-pitted old iron rod. The thing was about a foot and a half long and one end was rusted to a point. In the building was the surprise. A brand new, dark-green Chevrolet sedan. With the apple in one hand and the iron rod in the other, Norman had just made his third circle of inspection around the car when his father arrived in the doorway.

Mr. Woods was not at all pleased to see three brand-new scratches all the way around his brand-new car. Without thinking Norman had held the rod out at arms length with the end touching the car as he made his rounds.

"Give me that thing," his father commanded. The tone of voice brought the boy to reality. He dodged the outstretched hand. His dad made a fast move to get the piece of iron. Norman mistook this move as trouble. He ran. Mr. Woods ran too. As the parental hand was reaching for Norman's collar, the kid dove under the barbwire fence. In a second he was on his feet and going northeast as fast as he could. The goal was Sam's house across the road. There were four fences to cross when they bee-lined it straight to the neighbour's. Each fence gave the youngster an advantage of a few yards while his father climbed over them.

Woods Junior had Sam's porch doorknob in his hand when that big hand was firmly grasping his collar. Sam came to the door with a questioning look on his face.

"This kid just scratched up my new car," panted Woods Senior.

"That is sure enough reason to give him a licking, but not in my house Tom. You'll have to wait till you get home to do that. But come in both of you, come in."

The outcome was that Sam brought out wine for the men, Orange Crush for the little guest. Later the Woods men walked home hand in hand on the road.

Norman told me, "I've liked Sam ever since that time."

Thirty years ago, my brother-in-law and I were business partners. That is when he told me this story. Last night we went down the street two blocks, and had coffee with Joan and Norman. To get his approval, I asked him to read the bit about "Friends."

He read it and then turned to me and said, "Not quite true. We didn't go hand in hand. I wasn't that dumb. I stayed and had sardine sandwiches with Sam."

One More Gone

Raymond and Doris, after years of drought in the southern prairie, moved north to the edge of the forest to start over. Some crop land, a large pasture lease and cattle were the foundation of their new hope. It was Saturday night in the late spring. Most of the potholes in the country roads were drying up. Ed reined his horse in at Raymond's lane.

"Hi there, Ray. How's it going?"

"Hello Ed. Before you fall off that horse, better climb down and put him in the barn." With Ed's mount cared for and Ray's chores finished, they strolled toward the house.

Doris called out, "Hello Ed. You guys don't get coffee till I'm finished with the dishes."

At the wood pile, Ray leaned against the saw buck and rolled a cigarette. Ed sat on the chopping block, with his jackknife he reamed his pipe bowl.

"It sure is one beautiful evening."

"Yup, it sure is. And the mosquitoes aren't that bad." The neighbours smoked and made small talk.

"Would you believe it Ed? I lost a steer earlier this week."

"One of the yearlings that you wintered in that south pen over there?" Ed puffed out a blue cloud of smoke. "What happened to it? Did it just up and die?"

Ray answered, "Heck no. It just up and disappeared."

"You can't find a trace of it?"

"No sir. Not hide nor hair. It was here on Monday when I turned the cattle out in the north west quarter. I'm darn sure it's not in that pasture now."

"Before its pitch black out there you guys better come for coffee." Doris' voice faded away.

"Listen! Ray, that was one of your colts that whinnied."

"Sounded like it was over on the west side didn't it?" As the men silently waited for another sound, Ray continued, "What could be bothering the horses?"

When they were about to give up speculating and go for coffee, there was a new sound on the still night air. A rickety sounding car was making its way along the west side of the pasture. It proceeded to the corner, turned east and followed the trail on the north side of the pasture.

Ray wondered, "Where does he think he's going? There is water over the road up there." The men stood by the house, puzzled about the car that was heading for a big mud hole and trouble. The car stopped. The engine was shut off. All was silent on the north side of the pasture. Then BANG!

"That was a thirty-thirty," Ray said.

"Some nut out night hunting," Ed figured.

"Hunting Hell! My steers! Come on," yelled Ray.

Ray was moving fast. It took a bit of time for Ray to get a horse out of the corral and saddled. Ed had his horse cinched up and had the gate open to the pasture.

"Hey Ray, that guy is stuck. I can hear him racing his motor. Lead the way but don't leave me behind," Ed suggested.

Ray led the way at a fast gallop around the spruce bluff, through the aspens and across the willow swamp. At last there was open land, hard ground and good footing for the horses. The last part of the half mile ride was at a dead run, hooves drumming on the dry trail. The riders were a couple of hundred yards from the fence when the car drove away. At a distance from Ray and Ed, the driver turned on his lights, and sped away. Gaining the south west corner of Ray's pasture, the driver stopped for a few minutes then went on into the night. The friends rode home.

Ed remarked, "You know Ray, when you were catching your horse I thought I heard a shot out west, maybe like a .22. That guy with the car was making the noise when I was trying to hear."

"I'll be darned if I know what it's all about," Ray summed up the whole situation. After sandwiches and coffee Ed offered, "If you want Ray, I'll stay over and help you look for your lost steer tomorrow."

Sunday morning was bright, clear and chasing away the dew. When the steer searchers finely got to the south west corner of the pasture, a few of their questions were answered. There in the grass was the remains of a field-dressed animal. The head and entrails of one of Ray's steers laid in the sunshine. It didn't take much sleuthing to tell that the carcass had been pulled by two people. The drag marks went under the fence and onto the road. That was the end. No more clues.

Monday morning was cloudy and threatening rain. The RCMP officer surveyed the scene of the rustlers' crime.

"The footprints are soft and too old for plaster casts." Then he continued, "The tire tracks are of old, worn out treads. That could mean any, or every car for miles around. When it comes right down to it, we don't have much proof of anything," the officer said.

Ray lifted his hat and with a finger or two of that same hand scratched his head. In a rueful voice he answered the police, "The only darn thing I can prove is there is one more steer gone."

Hard as Flint

In 1885, Swift Current, Saskatchewan was not a good place to look for employment. That was why Les's grandfather, who then was sixteen years old, hit the trail for Montana. There he took to frontier ranching like a duck to water.

Cattle, horses, desperadoes and six guns were common everyday things in his life. The ladder of success was there to climb, and climb he did. From green horn to top hand. This cowboy developed a way with outlaw horses and used a long rope on wild cattle. He waded into more than one saloon brawl with his six guns. He had learned how to use them well.

In time Granddad returned to Saskatchewan. He married Belle, and settled down to raise horses, cattle and a family. More years passed, their children grew to become adults and married. Granddad and Belle became Grandpa and Grandma. And Granddad kept the old habit of drinking his coffee from a saucer. It cooled much better than in the cup. Occasionally, when he was being really impolite, he would even slurp his coffee from the saucer.

During the long car trip to the wedding of a son, it was firmly impressed on Grandpa that booze and saucering coffee would not be allowed. Grandma did not consider these as acceptable social graces. Late in the afternoon on the day before the ceremony they arrived at the ranch home of the bride to be.

The father of the bride was delighted to meet another old cowboy. Talk about kindred spirits. To avoid the hustle and bustle of all the activity and all the people at the house, these gentlemen spent considerable time at the barns and corrals. They admired the saddle horses, assessed the few bulls that were at home, and generally got acquainted.

The refreshments for the wedding were in storage in a vacant bunk house. Now, pure reasoning would demand that these goods should be inspected, and even sampled. It would be absolutely unthinkable to serve putrid whiskey to guests on the morrow. They sampled it all. It passed inspection with flying colours and that was good. A cigar or two later with maybe another small taste, just to make sure it was still good, the bottle was capped. The supper gong sounded. The two gents were in a cheery frame of mind when they reached the house. They did walk straight and dignified, but there was an old time saloon fragrance about them.

In the ranch house dining room, Grandma was seated with the host at the head of the table. Around the square corner on her left was Grandpa. White porcelain cups on matching saucers were soon filled with coffee. Grandpa lifted his saucer with his right hand, with the left hand he dribbled coffee into the saucer. Grandma sat and looked daggers at her man. He continued with the coffee dribble. Grandma continued with the daggers. Dribble... Daggers...

Grandpa, with the cold dignity of his gun fighting days, said, "Belle, if you say one word, I'll slurp it."

Lonesome

Once we were out of the city, we could see stars through the broken clouds. The crisp, cold air of the October morning was made to order for elk hunting. Jack had picked me up at 4:30 a.m. My cased rifle was under the front of the seat. A container of sandwiches and some odds and ends of clothes took up the rest of the space on the seat. I admired the long red hood on my friend's new 52 Ford half-ton. The drone of the defroster soon made me unbutton my wool jacket. Then I bestirred myself to ask about our destination.

Jack explained, "We go west to Lundbreck, then north, some miles up that road we'll come to a stream. On the far side of that, there's a trail going up to the Porcupines. There's about 3 inches of snow. That'll make for good tracking. Tonight we'll have our game dressed and be on our way home." For a few miles we talked of the good old 30.06. His new Winchester was much like my gun.

It was close to the mountains that we found an eating spot that was open. After a plate of pancakes, eggs and sausage, we were ready for some serious hunting. Out in the parking lot, Jack studied the sky as he fished for his truck keys.

"I do believe we have a Chinook coming."

By the feel of the air I was sure the Chinook was already there. We reasoned that farther north it might not melt so soon. Away we went. Miles farther, there was a hay field that paralleled the road for a half a mile. It had been worked up to reseed. There were black lumps shining through the snow. Darn it! It was thawing. At the creek we made a fast turn around. The bright sun over the Porcupine Mountains meant we could have trouble getting back to the highway. As we reached the more level road, we relaxed a little bit.

When we got to the hay field, it was a shining black mess of mud. There, just across the fence, was a man on foot. He wore a woolen jacket, a well used Stetson, scarred chaps, and under the mud I suppose he had boots. He was of an average build, looked to be a local rancher.

We stopped. He took a handful of dry grass and wiped some of the mud off his right side. From boots to Stetson he had slid in the dirt.

We offered him a ride and he climbed in the cab with us. Our Hello was sort of wasted. He seemed to prefer silence to dumb questions, like what happened. At the south end of the field stood a bay horse. The saddle and whole right side of the animal was covered with the same stuff that was on our passenger. This guy held up a hand as a signal to stop. With a smile he said, "Me and my horse are temporarily estranged."

Homesteading

Within the western provinces of Canada, each square mile is divided into four quarters. Most of this soil became owned by farmers through homesteading. There was C.P.R. land, Hudson Bay land, school land, South African Script, and Métis Script. This land did not fall in the homestead category and was only a small percentage of the total area, but it did add to the confusion of the land seeker. To locate a homestead in itself was sometimes a gigantic undertaking. It took money to hire a land locator. By the time some of the hopeful searchers had reached our part of Saskatchewan, they had just enough cash to pay the ten-dollar fee at the land office and eat for a few days.

Sam hired a team and guide at Morse, Saskatchewan to show him land south of Notakue Creek. It was a trip of about fifty miles one way. They arrived at the general area at sundown. The land was flat and fertile. The rich stand of grass was proof of its worth. After unharnessing the horses and feeding them, they were tied to the side of the buckboard. Mr. Finley and his chauffeur ate their lunch. In the dark they got into their bed roles for a nights sleep. In the gray dawn, the horses were molested by mosquitoes. The team broke their halters and went home to find shelter in the livery barn at Morse.

When the dust settled at the rig, the men saw their horse power disappearing over the ridge. The team was going northeast at a full gallop.

"I am going to walk to the Walsh Brothers ranch, and get a ride to town. I'll come back and get you and the buggy."

"When will that be?" asked Sam.

"Well, as soon as I can make it," said the guide. "If you want to walk to the ranch, it's about twenty-five miles that way." The guide waved his arm in a northeasterly direction.

The prospective homesteader spent the next few hours locating the survey stakes of his desired farm. That job done, he followed in the same direction as the teamster had taken earlier. At the creek he found narrow banks and deep water. He was not sure which way to go to find the crossing that they had used the day before. When he did find the spot, he waded across. To get to the ranch and get a ride with his driver become his goal. To stop and dry out his patent leather shoes had not occurred to the hiker. Mile after endless mile Sam walked in utter solitude. This was so unlike the English countryside. This tall robust gentleman walked hurriedly. Late in the afternoon the man-made material of his shiny black shoes had all but deteriorated. That didn't allow for much foot comfort.

Cresting a hill a few miles south of Wiwa Creek, he saw a streak of dust on the north side of the valley. Only four miles away was the hoped-for ride to the railroad, and he had missed it.

Grandfather Brotten left Swift Current on foot. In two days of walking he found nothing like his Norwegian homeland. Fifty miles and only hills and shallow valleys. At last, coming to some pink granite boulders, he stopped to mop his brow. These big rocks were the closest thing to home that he had seen. Oh, but it was hot and dry! Wandering into a nearby coulee, he found cold clear water trickling out beside a rock. After a refreshing drink of water he knew that he had found his land. It had taken two days to come out this far, but it only took one day to get back to the land title office. There was the fear that someone would file for homestead rights on this parcel by just looking at the map. His grandson Kevin still appreciates that spring in his pasture.

Andrew Muri selected his land by driving with a team and wagon along the approximate east side of the section. Covered by the cured gray prairie grass, the land looked rather flat. It came as a surprise when he walked across his new homestead and found a deep ravine that occupied one quarter of his land. That's why he had to start a cow herd. His great grandsons, Russell and Scott, are cattlemen.

Gus Johnson arrived at Herbert from Sweden via Oklahoma. He spent his first winter on the prairie at the Nybo stopping house. For most of the winter, he would leave at dawn and return at dark. He inspected an incredible amount of land while he wore out two pairs of four-buckle overshoes. In March he returned to the Moose Jaw Land Title Office and claimed his homestead, land that was two miles west of where he had stayed for the winter.

No one could ever imagine the number of miles that were walked, or driven, or ridden with a penciled township map on a scrap of brown paper as the only aid in locating a new home.

One of Jim Ketter's ancestors left France, bound for America. After a number of years in New York city, he had become totally Americanized. Then the call of free land in Canada was heard. He answered the call. A land locator in Saskatoon, Saskatchewan was helpful to the limit. Jim's forebearer was at the hotel door at daybreak. The locator met him as arranged.

"My man will be here very soon with the democrat."

That's when the transplanted Frenchman from the U.S. blew up.

"Never in all my days have I had anything to do with the Democrats. I have voted Republican every time."

They smoothed his feathers, and found him land.

Tall Grass

The way I smiled at the mirror, I was practically guaranteed a good day. I pulled on my boots, set my hat at a jaunty angle and went out to greet the dawn. But say, it is cool out this morning. A boss's-heart-kind-of-day, the boys used to call a cold day, just to bug me a little bit. I went inside with a feeling for toast and coffee.

My lifetime partner asked, "Is the lawn mower ready to go?"

"No, it will need a lot of attention before we cut the lawn."

"Well, I wish you would get it going and trim up this grass."

"But dear, the lawn is not ready to be cut."

"Aw come on now, its looking very scruffy."

I argued, "It's only along the walks and the side of the garage that it's high enough to cut."

"That's where it looks the worst, but it should all be cut."

"But dear I like the looks of the high grass. When the leaves are wide and curving down, they look so good." Then a better line of reasoning occurred to me. "If we had five thousand acres of grass like this, we would still have cows."

"But we haven't got cows anymore, so this mess has to be cleaned up," demanded my friend.

"Don't you appreciate the natural look of grass? When it's headed out and has that seed cluster on top it sure looks good. Do you remember how good it was to pull a long stem of grass, and chew while you leaned on the corral rail to look at a pen of cows?"

"That's in the past and I do not chew on grass stems," she said.

"Anybody that would cut grass off an inch long, would also be the kind of person that would roach the main on her horses, and go in for all kinds of unnatural foofraw."

"I know some old-timer that could get his boot heels shot off. And a good swat with a spade would put the crown of his hat down close to that vacuum chamber that's so full of sentiment over some long ago, defunct cows and long grass."

I thought "Suffer'n cats! This was supposed to be a good day."

Memory Lane

I had sold the business to Armand, Norman and Leon, but still stopped in quite often. Dollard was a few minutes early for his appointment. The micro chips in his car were giving the fuel pump the wrong messages. It took a long time to get it convinced to go to work in the morning.

"Something like a spoiled horse," was his diagnosis.

"Instead of standing here, let's go to the coffee room," I suggested. As we sat at the table with our cups, the conversation flowed along like you would expect from two seniors that were out of step with modern technology.

"When you have trouble, it's no use lifting the hood. There is so darn much stuff crammed in that space that you can't see anything," I said.

"And even if you could see the trouble, what could you do about it with all the modern junk in there. I don't know what it's good for," Dollard replied.

"I've heard that it's for pollution and better gas mileage. But what you save in gas, you pay for many times over when you put in new electrical gimmicks," was my thought.

"And these kids that put on big tires and raise the truck a foot or two, are asking for trouble," I said.

"Ya, they don't realize that monster trucks have thousands of dollars of extras beside tires and blocks," thought Dollard. He added, "When we were young, we never had trouble like that. 'Bout all we had back then were horses."

"Ya, I remember those days," I said. "About the only problem back then was if the horse decided to run away on you. Then you had problems." I continued, "You had horses, so you must have had runaways."

The memory brought a chuckle. "Oh boy, did I have runaways! I had lots of horses and lots of runaways." My friend continued, "I had a team of bay mares, they were fairly light weight but strong and a lot of spark too. I could let them out of the barn one at a time, with harness and bridles on, and they would go and take their place at the sleigh pole and wait to be hitched up. Around home they were kittens, but when I got a half mile from town two men could not hold them in. They wanted to run like crazy. And when I left town, it was the same thing. They would want to run flat out. I was always lucky if I didn't upset at the corner at the edge of town. A half a mile down the road, and these mares were back to being kittens again."

"One night, we were at a dance at Penn School. There was a whole sleigh full of us. It took four men to hitch the horses up while I held the lines. Every time I drove them to a dance, you would think that they were the ones that got drunk. That night, when we left the school, we were on a dead run for the half mile on the road north. When we came to the corner to go to Spruce Creek, we had way too much speed. The box got tipped off the sleigh and everyone got spilled out. I slid along on my belly for a long, long way at the end of the driving lines before I got them stopped. Then I had to go back and get the sleigh box loaded and everyone in again."

"A team like that could surely add colour to a dull life, couldn't they?" I said.

"When times got better, I sold that team. Then I got the tractor."

We sat and sipped coffee in silence and remembered.

"It sure was boring driving a tractor after you were used to horses," Dollard mused.

"Yes, if you had a hundred horses, you would find that each one had its very own personality," I figured. "With the tractor, if it ran, it was good, If it didn't, you most likely had a heck of a costly repair bill."

"Yes, if a horse wouldn't work, it was a matter of figuring out what was wrong, and sometimes that was a challenge." Dollard summed it up, "That one team I had were showoffs, but just the same, they were a pleasure to own. A person should have been hung for parting with horses like that."

All I could add was, "Amen."

Our Mistake

Do you remember Spike heels? I bet that you don't remember Cuban heels. They were shorter, and only about half as high as the Spike. The thing that gave them the fashion banner was the squareness. From the rear, or heel section of the lady's shoe, the heel was blended in with the natural shoe shape, but the sides of the heel were hewed or cut straight, parallel to the line of travel if the wearer was not bow legged or pigeon toed. The back of the heel was cut at a 90-degree angle to the side. This made the square heel track of a lady.

It was a chilly day in the late autumn. We students, at rural Nybo School, District #3006 in October 1936 were smart enough to close the door on a cold day.

There was a gasp of breath from one of the big girls. From another part of the room came a shriek. The general disruption of the room caused James to look up from his studies. It caused me to stop counting the number of V-joint boards between the blackboard and the ceiling, which was not part of my grade five math studies.

Most of the girls had their feet tucked under them on their desk seats. One or two were standing on their desk seat.

Then James and I were given the mandate, "James and Bernard KILL THAT MOUSE!" James watched the furry, gray invader who had upset the feminine members of our small educational community, while I hustled to the cloak room for two corn brooms. The chase began. Right past the teacher's desk, behind the piano, under the row of grade one desks, and to the stove.

This coal burning monster was surrounded with a heat shield (actually, this ornate stamped metal circular wall with the huge door was more of a kid protector). This shield gave us a problem for a bit. We beat on the side of the stove shell until the noise drove the mouse out.

"There it goes," screamed a feminine student.

"KILL THAT MOUSE!" screamed the teacher. The mouse was rested by this time, so we had another good run. My pal and I knew that we had the stage. We played it to the hilt. Another trip around the room and I had the little critter cornered.

"Don't kill him," James whispered. "If we do, we'll have to go back to our desks."

"KILL THE MOUSE!" The tone was authoritative. The next pause was at the front of the classroom, near the cloakroom door. We had our brooms in a good defensive position. The mouse was cornered again. But there came the teacher with enough momentum that she slid straight legged with her right Cuban heel out in front. It contacted the mouse, who was huddled against the wall right in the corner, with no escape route. The mouse was spread over a large area.

"All right boys, clean it up."

While we cleaned James muttered, "We didn't do this right."

Moving

We sold the cull cows, the yearlings and the bulls. Four days later we sold the brood cows. Next went the last of the hay. A month later the machinery was sold. The leases were cancelled and we were no longer ranching. The deal was that we would stay and look after the yard until fall.

In October our house was built in town. We both drove to town every day, but our work patterns were not the same. Berniece would drive the car or half ton and take in a small load of household stuff. I would use the 3/4 ton and take in more stuff. I thought that we were doing just fine with this method. It didn't take up much of the day loading or unloading.

Until my wife said, "This is it. Our stuff is so scattered, we can't live at the ranch or in town. Tomorrow, I'm going to take the day off and finish moving our things into the house."

I tried every angle to stay with our old system but I lost. We had the washer and drier on my truck, and a couple of beds and mattresses on her truck. The dresser from the spare room was to go on her load. Sure as heck, all of the tools were in town – no screwdriver to use to take the mirror off the dresser.

"Let's put it on my truck the way it is."

"But will that be safe?" asked my better half.

"Oh sure. I'll drive slow so the wind won't catch it. It will be Okay." Talk about confidence! I watched the dust cloud she raised on the way to town.

I poked along very leisurely. It was a bright autumn morning and I was really enjoying the beautiful scenery that northern Saskatchewan can offer at that time of year. I forgot about the mirror. Four miles from town I must have been progressing right along. Bang! It sounded like a shot gun. There was our fancy mirror lying face down on the west bound lane of the highway, in a million pieces too. In town I got a pail, broom and shovel, and returned to the place that I was not proud of. The splinters of glass that had any size to them picked up easily, the tiny flakes were impossible to sweep up. I did the best I could with the mess and went back to town. There was not much conversation about the mirror. Maybe she had figured it a goner when I loaded it.

As the days went by, I could see the little specks of my mirror moving west on the road to Chitek Lake. I suppose that the passing tires would move the glass. Before the snow came, the bits of mirror had moved about three hundred yards west. The next spring I saw some of my shiny stuff on the highway east of Lloydminster, Saskatchewan.

Grandma told me, with a swat to my britches when I was a little kid, that if I did something bad it would surprise me how far it would spread. Sure enough, the following summer I think I saw bits of my mirror on the road just east of Vancouver.

Pie Face

On the evening of April 4, 1938, Basil called me on the phone. "Would you care to come and help me ride Pie Face tomorrow?" "Sure thing. What time should I be there?" I asked.

After a big bunch of teenage conversation that the world could have done without, our plans for the morrow were in place. Pie Face was a three-year-old black filly with a large white spot on the front and side of her head. She looked like she had been the victim of a cream pie in the face gag. The fact that Pie Face was well halter broke, was certainly in our favour. She had been tied in the barn and handled to the point of being considered a pet. Basil had his saddle on Lady, a wise middle-aged bay mare. We put my saddle on the black filly and led her out to the water trough.

When she finished her drink, I slowly tightened the latigo. As the cinch snugged up to a tension that would keep the saddle in place, there was a volcanic action. Pie Face jumped over the end of the water trough. At the height of that leap, my saddle was a bit above the lower shingles on the pump house roof. Basil was mounted on Lady and it only took a few moments until he brought the runaway back.

Con, the hired man, helped me get on this frisky pony. Basil had her snubbed to his saddle horn with about two feet of rope. Away we went. Whenever Pie Face would try to buck, Lady hurried her along a little faster. After six miles of this travel both horses were warmed up, my mount being by far the warmest. Basil handed me the halter shank that he had been towing Pie Face with. We were on our own. I was riding Pie Face and she acted so educated.

As we stopped in front of the barn, Con came out. He said, "Let me hold her head, and you get off real slow so you don't spook her. Spoiled horses are too easy to come by."

After supper we curried and brushed the newly broke saddle horse.

"Don't comb out her mane and tail. She's not ready for that just yet," Uncle Albert advised us. The next morning, being Sunday, April

6 and Aunt Emma's birthday, we were going to take Pie Face for a short ride before we went to the birthday party. Pie Face had such good manners that we could hardly believe our skill as horse breakers. As a caution we did snub her to Lady as we had done the day before. Oh did she ever ride nice.

On Saturday night we had a sharp frost. The dirt lumps on the cultivated field made for careful stepping by our mounts. I had been on my own for a short way, and the pony was behaving nicely.

"I'll turn one way and you go the other way and we will meet and go home," Basil suggested.

Part way into my half circle Pie Face stopped, looked around and saw that she was not snubbed to Lady. Then she exploded! The second or third jump, and I was a goner. To figure how high in the air my boots were, you have to add the height of the mare, the height the mare jumped, the length of the halter shank, the stretch of my arm and the length of my body. That's where my boots were. Gravity brought me down in a jiffy, on my back on the frozen dirt lumps. How could a person, landing on ones back, believe that he had broken every little bone in his body?

At the birthday party, to my embarrassment, word got out that I had gotten bucked off but good. Lloyd Myers, whose trade was rodeo saddle bronc riding, comforted me with a pat on my aching shoulder and said, "That's all right kid. That's just part of growing up."

Years later on the ranch, I had cut a number of Red Tamarack posts. These were eight feet long and eight to ten inches across the top and green wood. One post at a time was all that I could drag out of the muskeg on the end of a lariat with a good saddle horse on the other end. This pile of posts got plopped in a low spot in the yard. The top ones were heavy and the ones on the ground were frozen in and heavier, but I got them moved to a better spot.

The next morning was April 6, nearly fifty years after riding Pie Face. I sat on the edge of the bed. Oh how my back and shoulders ached. Then I recalled Lloyd Myers comforting words. I thought to myself, "Maybe I'm still growing up."

189

A Wee Bit O' Privacy

They were Grace's Grandpa and Grandma. Their first names could have been Mac and Mary. They lived in Scotland. Mac tended a steam engine in a local factory. The engine was stationary and at times the job seemed to be the same way. Mary tended their young family. Her job was much more active. That she had medical problems was certain, but the comely young lady made the best of her lot.

In 1880 the lure of Canada was spread over Europe. Mac and Mary emigrated to the new world. Arriving in Toronto, they were greeted, "Hoot Mon!". The emigration officer was also Scotch. "You being a man of steam, you will be needed on the great railroad to the west." Mac knew nothing about locomotives, but with his steam engine experience he was more knowledgeable than any other applicant for the position of CPR engineer.

As the rails were laid west, Mac proudly drove the smoking locomotive. Mary moved west with her husband to live on the frontier. When the railroad was completed and in full operation, living took a more settled manner.

A little board shack on the prairie at the edge of Medicine Hat became home to Mac, Mary and family. This was not a pretentious house, but after all, this was the Alberta District of the Northwest Territories. This grand new land was in the first stage of development. At the start, a few minor discomforts were no big thing.

Mac would be hooting in with his train from Calgary in the small hours. Mary, getting ready for bed, removed her false teeth and dropped them in the small dish on her dresser. After blowing out the lamp, she saw two native ladies looking in the uncurtained window. "Curious, but friendly Indians," she said to herself as she got into bed.

The following night Mary was surprised to see that she had a large audience at her bedroom window. She removed her dentures, put out the light and went to bed in the dark. Night number three, Mary had a tremendous gathering at her window. She carefully brushed her red hair, then set the lamp on a stand next to the window. Removing her dentures brought out the oohs and ahhs of the watchers out in the moonlight. With her back to the window, Mary popped out her glass eye and put it on the bit of paste that she had earlier put on her hand mirror. Swinging around with a flourish she held the mirror close to the window pane. The lamp illuminated the all seeing evil eye. The watchers close to the house had no escape other than to stampede over their comrades. The mob sorted themselves out and raised the dust as they ran across the prairie.

Mary cleaned up her eye and the mirror, and gained her wee bit o' privacy.

Profit

It was a blistering hot summer day. His combine repair would be ready in a couple of hours, so Uncle Albert strolled into the Imperial Hotel. Opening the door to the beverage room, he heard the hum of many voices. The place was crowded. It seemed that everybody had taken refuge from the sun in this exact spot.

"Hey you, come sit down." The invitation came from one of the two gray haired Métis gents. "I'm John. This is my brother Joe." With that, he pushed a chair out with his foot.

"Thanks. My name is Albert."

"You from Shaunavon?" asked Joe.

"No. I farm north of Vanguard."

John waved a burly arm to order a round of drinks. "We used to have a friend lived out that way. Good cowboy. Name Ted. You know about him?"

"Yes, he was my brother-in-law." Albert said.

"Where is he at now?" Joe asked.

"Ted died in Vancouver a few years ago."

With a long face John said, "You make me sad to tell me that." Joe and John sat very still for a few moments. It seemed as this was a minute of reverend remembering. John bestirred himself. To his deep brown eyes there came the light and brilliance of youth.

"I'll tell you about Ted. Me and Joe sat at that table right over there between door and window. Ted come in. I holler, 'Hey you.' Ted come here. We all shake hands." John sipped at his glass. "I said, 'Too bad you ain't got your rigging here. Me and Joe need help.' Ted just laugh and say, 'When do you guys need help to clean up a table of beer." Then he sit down and have one. "No, Me and Joe gonna take the train to Maple Creek. Gonna bring forty fifty horses to place south of the lake."

"When are you going?" Ted asked.

Joe knew the answer, "Soon as this place run out of beer."

John had more exact timing. "We take the late train, get there early in the morning."

"Well, lets go. I got my outfit over at the station. I'm packed up for Alberta. Going out for spring roundup," Ted answered.

The brothers together, "You got a job for sure?"

"Yup, and I got my ticket for Calgary. So lets go get them bromtails home before I go."

The three horse wranglers dozed away the very early morning hours in the Canadian Pacific Railway station in Maple Creek. In due time they were driven out to the ranch to receive the band of horses.

"Supposed to be three broke saddle horses. Which one's them?"Joe wanted to know.

"I got mine," shouted John. His lariat loop settled on the neck of a big bay mare that had saddle marks. "You guys can have what's left."

It was past noon by the time the horse herd was strung out going east.

"Ted, I bet you two bits you can't ride that blaze face sorrel." John wagered. "Well not 'til I get my saddle on him." Ted took the bet.

John roped the sorrel. Joe got a halter on him and used his jacket for a blindfold. Ted saddled the animal and got set deep in the saddle. John handed over the halter rope. Joe jerked off the blindfold. The wild horse started out like he was going to climb stairs with its front feet, then changed to high lurching bucks. Instead of spurring, Ted slapped with his hat and yelled like a demon. This convinced the brute to run. Out on the open prairie Ted and mount raced in a great big circle. As the circles became smaller, the horse slowed down. In a short while all three were riding together, as common place as you please.

"You got to ride that horse til we find you 'nother one." Joe made that rule.

John made the next ride. Then Joe had his turn. Then came Ted's chance. Each ride was based on a twenty-five-cent bet. This style of life carried on for the entire eighty miles of travel.

"Bet you two bits John, if you ride that black gelding he'll buck stiff legged. I'll cover all four hoof tracks in one shot with my hat brim,"

Ted offered. There was the usual rope it, get it down, halter it, blindfold it, snub it to another horse, saddle it, mount it and when John said, "Turn em loose" the black gelding exploded with an angry roar. A burst of power sent him forward and up. Way up. Then straight, stiff, front legs he came down. This seemed to be the only technique the horse was going to use to gain freedom from the saddle and the crazy nut hollering WHOOPPEEE WHOOPPEE. At each jarring contact with the ground, John had his feet forward in the stirrups, and toes out. As they again started for the sky, John spurred, and yelled WHOOPPEE. Joe and Ted calmly rode from one set of hoof prints to the next. The results were always the same. "No Ted. Don't take your hat off to measure them tracks, too far apart."

The trip never did get boring, but ended successfully at the corral of the owner of the horse herd. This gent asked, "Which three did you ride?" With an offhanded air John answered, "All of em."

When the wranglers were delivered back to Swift Current, and their wages paid, the brothers were about to divide the few dollars in three. An equal share for Ted.

He declined. "No, that was your job and there wasn't much profit. You guys need the money, besides I'm going to work." Joe sipped his drink. "That Ted, he was one good guy."

John made a fist with thumb out, and poked Albert in the hip. With the grin of an imp he motioned toward his brother. "You should seen Joe. Me and Ted bet two bits Joe can't ride little white mare. She's small, maybe seven fifty, eight hundred pounds. She's old, long teeth. Ted snub and I pull blindfold. Joe, he ready for good buck. Only horse I see do that. She slump down like fall on her belly, then swoosh she run backwards so fast Joe go forward and get saddle horn in gut. He soon get his face out of horse main, and set up. Then white mare jump sideways like jackrabbit, then run. I laugh so hard my horse get away. Ted laugh so his horse try buck him off. He catch my horse. We catch Joe after while."

Albert shook his head. "Two of you guys riding green broncs and the other one on a bucking horse, and no one to ride pick-up. What if you had trouble?"

That question had never occurred to John.

With a chuckle John explained, "We was slim, and strong and young then."

Joe confirmed that thought, "Fifty years ago, we was rawhide cowboys."

When you stop to consider the gain, I suppose Ted got the most. When you have helped to build a memory that lasts a half a century, who could beat that for profit.

Santa

Ray, Lawrence, Dennis and Leo met at the grain elevator office. Lawrence was the local agent and the organizer. It took a while to get the Santa suit and equipment sorted out. It took longer to get Leo dressed to perfection, because he was perfection itself. No detail was overlooked. Everything was in readiness.

Dennis was a hi-for-to-go guy from a way back. He had found the miniature Santa sleigh at an auction sale. It was just the size to follow behind a snow machine. This Santa conveyance was hitched to Dennis's machine and the route was reviewed. It was two blocks to the hospital, and a quick round of the wards, then six blocks to the school to preside at the Children's Christmas Party. Then they would go back to the elevator office for a quick snort and to undress Santa.

On their Ski Doos, Lawrence and Raymond (friends along for the ride) followed Dennis, who was towing Santa Claus in the one man sleigh. Leo was rehearsing his "HO HO HOs," when Dennis made much too fast a turn at the T-intersection of the hospital corner. There was no choice! They had to turn. The sleigh skidded sideways and hit a frozen rut, then overturned. Santa was catapulted out in a graceful arcing dive that ended head first in the deep snow beside the road. All three machines stopped close to the accident. Their drivers watched Santa straighten up. "You ----, crazy, stupid, ----, idiot! You —, reckless, ----! Were you trying to kill me? What a damn mess!" was Leo's first reaction.

The second was to shake some of the snow out of his coat. When the toque and beard were pulled out of the snowbank, and the bifocals hung back on the local Santa Claus's face, the party returned to the grain company office for repairs.

In a nearby home that aligned with the street that Santa had just travelled, a five-year-old gentleman, all scrubbed and dressed for the school party, went to the front step. He was viewing the northern sky with the hope that he might, just might, see Santa up among the stars. Unbelievably there he was right on the corner of their front lawn. He rushed inside, a look of astonishment on his face. "I REALLY SAW SANTA CLAUS!"

"Did you see his sleigh?" his Dad asked rather offhandedly.

"Uh huh," the little guy said.

"Did you see his reindeer?" The father asked still in a casual manner. He didn't realize the importance of this actual sighting.

"No. I guess they ran away when the crazy, stupid, idiot ran into the sleigh with his Ski Doo."

"Then what happened?" asked the Mother who had just entered the room. The little guy was all fired up, but when Mom joined in, it made him stop and think. If it had been man to man, he could have told his Dad the forbidden words.

"Santa said some bad words. The man tied the sleigh behind his Ski Doo, and Santa got in. Another man said, "Its all right Santa, a needle and thread, and a good stiff drink will fix you up.""

Movie Script

My entire movie knowledge was gained by going to the western shows at the Elks hall on Saturday nights. In that day and age a movie had to have four sections;

1. Beginning of some sort.
2. The wounded hero.
3. Revenge.
4. Happiness ever after.

A few years ago I lived through a real life show like that. Mind you it was a very, very low budget thing.

Section 1

Our community hall at Leoville, Saskatchewan was condemned. A small but active town needs a center for things like suppers, dances, bingos, meetings and whatever. Against seemingly impossible odds, funds were being collected so we could build a new hall.

Section 2

The phone rang. I dropped my hammer and dolly, left the truck fender I was repairing and went to the office to take the call.

"Good morning. This is Joe. I represent The Unbelievable Good Advertising Company from Montreal. I am calling to give your business a terrific boost. But first, let me tell you that this large favour I am about to offer you includes a free trip of your choice to either the Bahamas, Hawaii, or Acapulco. All you have to pay for are your lunches and dinners. The breakfasts are free. Also included are seven days use of a u-drive car. Totally free with one tank of gas. The flight is free but you of course will pay for the hotel room. All that you have to do to qualify for these free gifts is to place an order for three hundred and fifty advertising pens. We'll print your business name and address and your phone number on each pen absolutely free. Oh yes, the pens are the bankers' quality, slim trim model.

I interrupted, "It's too bad you called, because I can't leave the shop to go flying around the Caribbean or Mexico."

"Oh, but did I tell you the free trip is transferable? You could give it to one of your staff, or a customer, or anyone you choose. I will put all the documents in with the pens and send them COD. You fill in the trip forms and return them with a small registration fee, and in just a few days some lucky person and friend will be gone on a fabulous holiday. Oh yes, which hotel will you choose?"

After he named four or five, I made a pick, "Southern Holiday sounds good to me." By this time I had decided to go for the deal and give the trip to the hall fund for a raffle.

About ten days later there it was! Sure enough, a COD for Four Hundred and Nineteen Dollars. I paid the Post Mistress, rushed back to the shop and opened the carton of treasures. One quarter of the pens would not write. A big bunch of those that would write were so scratchy they were useless. Onto the free trip papers! It was a shock to learn that the hotel I had chosen was to cost TWELVE HUNDRED BUCKS for six nights, and the meals were about half as much. Reading on I learned that the small registration fee was $39.95 and to transfer the trip to another party would cost a further $89.95.

"Who would want to pay nearly two thousand dollars for a free trip?" I asked myself. A call to Montreal informed me that the aforementioned company was no longer in business. I knew then that I was wounded.

Section 3

The year that the new community hall was finished, my phone rang. "Good afternoon, this is Joe calling from the Very Good Advertising Company." Before he got too far into his pitch, I got his address. Checking the note pad that I had used when I bought the bankers trim line model pens, I learned that this company was two doors down the hall from the one that sold me the no-write scratchers. I felt sure that I was talking to the same guy.

"Do we have a great offer for you! With the purchase of forty genuine leather coasters, or eighty key tags with your company name or logo stamped in gold colour, for four hundred and nineteen dollars, we will give your wife or girlfriend a fur coat, a diamond necklace and a diamond broach." He caught his breath and went on. "The coat is from Hollywood Furs Incorporated, is made of rabbit fur and is a beautiful garment. Did you see the picture 'White Limousine'? Effee Lamourmore, the star in that show, wore that same style and make of coat. She certainly looked elegant and charming."

"No, I guess I missed that one," I had to admit. This call came in a bit after 2:30 P.M. I had to know all and every bit about each teeny little detail. "Was it a rabbit skin coat? Was it white or brown rabbit? Would the hair fall out and leave a trail of rabbit when she wore the coat? How big were the diamonds? How many diamonds were there in the necklace? What was the broach made of? How many diamonds in it? How big were they?" The boys came into the office for their three o'clock coffee break. I still had questions to ask. At 3:30 we had all the fine points settled. It was time for him to close the deal.

"What will it be, the key holders or the coasters?" he asked. "I'll send them COD."

"What is the address of your Saskatchewan branch?"

"We have no branches. Everything is handled right from here." It was near 3:45 by the time all the benefits of direct selling were explained to me. Joe must have thought that I was a bit thick between the ears. I thought to myself, 'It's now close to six o'clock in Montreal, Joe is late for supper. His wife or girlfriend will take a strip of off him pretty soon.'

"If you have no Saskatchewan address, I can't deal with you."

"But why? I told you we have only our Montreal office."

"Well Joe, if our deal went sour, I can't afford to come to Montreal to sue you. You have to have a Saskatchewan office." He banged down the phone so hard Ma Bell most likely had to replace it.

I lived happily ever after with two trim line bankers' model pens -- one nearly writes, the other one scratches.

The Sleigh

Walter had reached the lonely state of life. His wife had been dead for a year and now he lived alone. His sons and daughters were attentive, considerate and careful of their father's well being. One or another of the family would make a daily visit, but Walter still lived alone in his snug, one room cabin. There was a low fence of pine poles around the cabin to protect it from Walter's horses, and to discourage bull moose from rubbing their autumn antlers on the building.

On a sunny morning I met Edwin on the road. "Hey, you want a ride?" I asked.

"Sure I do. I have a few days off the job, so I thought I should come home and spend some time with Dad," Edwin said when he got settled in the pick up truck with me.

"It's only a couple miles off the road, so I may as well run you up to Walter's," I offered.

"Thanks I'd appreciate that," he said.

When we got to Walter's place, he welcomed me, directed me to a chair and handed me a large granite cup of tea. That tea cup must have held most of a litre and the full cup had a rainbow of colour on top. A gray-haired neighbour of Walters sat in the corner nursing a similar cup. Something in the conversation caused our host to remember a deal of the past. Pacing the floor and with arm waiving and periodical chuckles, he told the story.

My brother Bill and I had cut birch planks and timbers to make a logging sleigh. We went to the conservation officer and got the Okay to take old sleigh irons that were on a little island in the muskeg, near where the town of Shell Lake is now. It was about a half a mile through the swampy ground to the island where a few burned stumps and the irons of seven sleighs were. Years before that, a logger left the sleighs there in the spring, and in the summer, a forest fire burned across the muskeg, and all that was left of the sleighs was the iron. The blacksmith used our wood and the iron we drug out of the muskeg and built a sleigh. When it was painted up, it sure looked good.

"How much do we owe you for the work?" I asked the blacksmith.

"If I can use your sleigh for two months to haul logs at Big River, I would call it even. I'll be home by Christmas time."

"That's a good deal for us because we don't need the sleigh until later," I said. We shook hands with the blacksmith and he took our sleigh to the logging camp at Big River.

A couple of weeks later, a Mounted Police came to our reserve looking for the Beads Brothers. When he found us, he gave us a summons to appear in court at Big River on July 2.

We were accused of stealing sleigh parts that belonged to the store keeper in Big River. He had seen the new sleigh and recognized the iron. Bill and I took a team and wagon and camped at Big River so we were there in time for the court.

We told the judge how we got permission to get the iron because it had been burnt over different times, and no one wanted it.

The store keeper said that it was his iron and he wanted it, and we stole his iron so he wanted our sleigh too. The judge was a sharp old boy. He fined us one dollar. He gave the store keeper two weeks to have every piece of the valuable iron to show the court the next time the judge was in town. If he did not do that we would get our dollar and sleigh back.

We loaded up with grub and drove to the edge of the muskeg where the iron was. We set up our tent and lived good. There was a spring with nice clear cold water a half a mile away. A week later, here came the store keeper. He waded into the slimy mud on his way to the island. We were in there when it was frozen. This man had a much worse trip. In a couple of hours he came out with two sleigh runner irons on his shoulder. He went to his wagon and ate some of a loaf of bread and drank from a small thermos. Then he went back for more iron.

The next time he came out, he wanted some of our tea. But we told him we would be camped there a long time and could not spare any food or drink. The third trip out he brought more pieces and was tired, dirty and bug bit. We raised our tea cups and said 'That's the way to go.

You are doing good.' It was dark when he came back again. He had ate his bread and had nothing left to drink.

He came over to our camp and begged for food. We had tea in the pail and stew in the pot. We offered him a meal in trade for his iron. That made him mad so he went and built a fire by his wagon, and sat there. He had no bed role or anything. Bill figured it was dumb of him to come forty miles without supplies. By daylight he was out again. That day he got the rest of the stuff loaded on his wagon. He was a mess, sunburnt, chewed by flies and mosquitoes. His clothes were tore up. He was cut and scratched. His face was red and he was weak. He had drank swamp water and got diarrhea. When the store keeper left the muskeg, we waved our tea cups and wished him a good trip home.

We were surprised at the trouble he went through to steal our sleigh.

A Prairie Town

A television anchor man was quoting an alderman. "The soul of our inner city area is..." and he carried on with the details. The news item in itself did not lodge in my memory, but it did make me ponder. Do cities receive souls upon conception? Is there an unlimited storehouse of souls to be given out to newly developed centers? Do small towns get souls too? Montreal and Vancouver did not start as large metropolitan centers, so if one of those had a soul, every little place would have one.

Long ago on our gently rolling prairie, beside Wiwa Creek, countless bison made their summer home. They departed and the grass was used by long-horned range cattle. They were replaced by people that turned the grass upside-down with their plows. Then the CPR grade crew with their countless horses, twenty dump wagons, plows, scrapers and big white tents came and built the foundation for a railroad.

When did our town of Hallonquist receive its soul? Or, did it have to wait until the two street town was fully developed, and a high, gray slab snow fence separated main street and the railroad?

When John S homesteaded, he had a thirty five-mile trip north to sell his grain and livestock. A few years later the rails were laid only sixteen miles to the south. That was progress. But now, ten years after starting his homestead, there was rail service only five miles from his front door. He could sell his grain at one of the three elevators, or load cattle at the new whitewashed stockyard. This was considered the ultimate in progress. John was proud of this new town in 1922.

One summer afternoon of that same year, John was at the CPR station to be right in the midst of the exciting activities. The first few months in the life of this town, every train day bordered on Mardi Gras. The unloading of passengers and express was exciting for the local people. This was the climax of their day! To the trainmen it was a bore, waiting for departure time.

205

"This is a dumb place to build a town," the blue-suited conductor said, within hearing of our John.

To correct this horrendous misconception, John felt it his duty to educate this worthy gentleman. With the patience and zeal of a missionary, he explained at great length the glory, growth and services of his new town. The conductor had heard it all before, many times in many places. He looked across the street to the false fronted two story hotel, that had as right and left neighbours, one story, false fronted store buildings. John concluded, "We have every thing you could need."

"And what would I do if this needed repair?" asked the railroad man as he palmed his big gold watch on his vest chain.

John wore a blue serge suit. He too, had a gold watch chain, and its timepiece was equal to the conductor's. John bought the watch before he left Pennsylvania to cast his future on the Canadian prairies.

"Our jeweller is qualified to work on railroad watches," was John's rebuttal.

"It is still a dumb place to build a town." The conductor still held his first opinion.

John's civic pride turned to anger. He bristled, jumped up and down and fairly shouted, "Good Heavens man, we even have a house of ill repute! What more do you expect?" John did not know that the two immoral women had come in one day and left the next. They too, found it to be a dumb place.

Nearly everyone went to town on Saturday night. Farmers bought repairs, their wives bought groceries, and their kids played hide and seek. The girls that had reached sophistication at fourteen, would gather in buggies or cars to share their secrets. It was the hub of the community. In the fall, threshing crews would arrive in grain wagons pulled by work horses. They came to replace worn out clothes and gloves. Some just visited. Others played pool. Still, others tried their luck at the green-covered table in the darkened shack behind the poolroom.

One teamster, with the last of his passengers loaded, backed his team away from the snow fence on the south side of main street. From the back end of the wagon box was heard, "I was lucky and played a smart game of poker, and I still lost everything. My whole twenty-two dollars." Miles from town, on the way home the luckless gambler gazed at the distant moonlit horizon and repeated for the umpteenth time, "I was lucky and played a smart game." He was interrupted by a chorus of voices, "Ya, we heard. Everything, the whole twenty-two dollars."

Seventy years later, the railroad, the hotel, the stores, the elevators are all gone. All that remains are the white church on the hill and the community hall.

On a sultry autumn day the soul of Hallonquist can gaze to the distant horizon and muse, "I was lucky and played a good game, but the conductor must have been right."

Mach 1

Winter, 1944, and war was raging over Europe and the South Pacific. This article appeared in a sedate magazine. The ever so truthful writing was about the first flight of a JET POWERED AIRCRAFT. Boy, oh boy, this was very heady stuff. It said the plane was straining, vibrating, and shaking badly. With a touch more thrust, it broke the sound barrier. Then the flight was smooth and soundless. Just going so fast, all noise was left far behind, gliding along faster than the speed of sound.

It seemed that the pilot had everything under control. Touching his upper lip, he felt his mustache. Now that was strange, no mustache. But it had grown for two years, ever since joining the Air Force and now it was gone. As the craft gained still more speed, this guy felt a pain in his right wrest. Well there it was the dog bite of eight years earlier. Imagine that blood dripping from every tooth mark.

By surpassing Mach 1, were we going back in time? Do you suppose the first man to fly that fast had time to worry about his appearance? Was he up above the clouds in a T-shirt, or did he scatter his togs around the cockpit while he examined a heeled-over dog bite? At the time, all we could do was shake our heads and mutter, "All of this new scientific stuff has more questions than there are answers for."

An autumn, Wednesday afternoon in 1981 was overcast and damp without rain. This is a perfect day to do some repairs to the corrals. I'd replace a few rails, fix the gates and cleanup in general. Things were progressing for me. The broken rails were replaced. The south gate was the next repair to do.

It was then that I heard the BOOM. This was not a fire arm, nor would it be a jet from Cold Lake Air Base. The sound was like that of a jet doing Mach 1, but a small edition. The bang came from the area of the natural salt lick. This is the spot, about three miles southwest of our yard, where the Indians go to shoot Moose. It was a puzzle with no quick and ready answer. I was getting along real good with my repair job, when one of our Cree neighbours came walking in from the southwest. He carried his 30.30 rifle under his arm. After the hellos were exchanged, he told me that he got between an old mother bear and her cub. With a dented cartridge in his magazine his gun jammed. The only thing he could do was run, which of course he did.

I looked this guy over really close. He looked the very same as he had the day before. The same wisp of gray at his temples, the same little wrinkles around his eyes. He had not gone back in time. I suppose, to get away from the mamma bear, he did make Mach 1 and that was the boom I heard.

Spike

Spike's mother was a gray bronco mare, one of forty head of horses some Alberta trader shipped into Hallonquist, Saskatchewan in 1936. At that sale, Carl Nelson Sr. was the high bidder on this mare. The only name she ever owned was Gray Bronco. She will always be remembered for two reasons, her unbelievable stamina, and when she was wearing a harness, she could explode without cause. This was a well put together horse, slick and smooth, weighing about eleven hundred pounds.

Spike's father was a Hackney stallion owned by Glen Gambol who lived north of Pambrun. This horse was a fancy stepping coach-type animal. Mr. Nelson bred five of his mares to this horse, with hope of getting a team or two that would get him over a long stretch of road in a short while. Of this family of colts, the only one that I got to know was Spike.

Spike was a long three year old about the time that I realized trading my saddle horse for a car was not smart. The roads drifted over with snow. That ended car travel. That was the reason for the trade I made with Carl's son, Jack Nelson, which was the use of Spike for the winter in exchange for all the education I could pile on the unbroken animal.

On a reasonable kind of winter day, Basil and I rode to Nelsons. I used my sister's horse for the one mile ride. Then, stripping my saddle off the old Thoroughbred and treating him like a dog, I slapped him and said, "Go Home." He went.

Jack had Spike tied in the barn. Jack, Basil and I stood in the gangway and studied this horse. Poor Spike, he had inherited his mother's disposition, his fathers barrel and chest, and his short thick legs must have been from the Ugly Fairy.

"Look at his feet! His mother must have been frightened by a snow shoe rabbit. They sure are big." Jack didn't use a sales talk about his horse.

I observed, "His head and hips match. Either one would fit a billy goat." As for colour, we could not be sure if he was black or brown.

The sun was sneaking toward the horizon by the time we got Spike out, saddled and snubbed to Basil's horse. When I mounted, he shook his head and started to halter pull. Basil moved his horse across in front of Spike. That changed his balance so we had to move forward through the gate into the pasture. Soon we were riding at a slow gallop. Then Spike changed his mind, instead of pulling back and fighting the halter, he decided to go somewhere else. He was handling his feet much like five running shoes in a clothes dryer. Basil let out enough rope so the horses were not running dangerously close together. We were circling to get back through the gate. This took us past the north slope of a small rise.

One slip and Spike was down on his side with my foot under his rib cage. The way I was pinned in, the horse had to make the first move to a standing position, but I was on my feet first. I looked at the tracks. ICE. "What the heck is ice doing on the north side of a hill in Saskatchewan in January?" The spill shook Spikes self confidence. He was much more careful with his feet. All straightened out, we were heading west, past the barn and to open country. It was considered a good idea to show this pony that there was more to life than grass and oat sheaves. Six miles later, there was but a bare thread of daylight left when we pulled up in front of Newton's barn.

Arling was closing the door when we rode up. He had just finished his night chores. When the sun set it had gotten quite chilly. My feet were cold and my ankle ached a bit, but nothing serious. It didn't take much coaxing to get us to stable our horses and stop for a bite to eat. When I stepped off that horse, my ankle wouldn't work. I was propped against the barn wall while my cousins took care of the horses. The walk to the house limbered up my foot to a point where I didn't limp to the table. After the meal was finished, both Aunt Emma and Uncle Ben thought that we should stay for the night. Aunt phoned her sisters to let them know that their boys were all right and would be staying for the night.

At the bunkhouse, it wasn't all right. The first try to remove my boot failed. I was not in favour of having the seam in the boot cut. With

211

one guy sitting on me and the other pulling on the boot, it came off. What a relief for a few seconds, then the old ankle ballooned to twice it's normal size. Arling said, "I'm going to get Mom to look at your foot."

I knew that Aunt Emma could doctor horses, cattle, sheep, people or any other ailing creature. "No it's too cold out. Don't bother her this evening," I resisted.

"It may be just as well if the folks didn't hear about this little fall right now," Basil reasoned. Arling surveyed the resources at hand, picked up a lotion bottle with enough for about four more shaves. He dribbled some on my ankle and massaged gently. Oh that hurt.

"Don't waste your shaving lotion like that." I was really begging him to stop.

He had a strong argument too. "We have to get the swelling down, because you can't ride in stocking feet this time of year."

A half hour passed and Basil figured it was time for the next treatment. He sat on my leg while Arling dumped the last of the lotion on my ankle and massaged again, but this time he used pressure. All I could do was to complain about how rough this pair of stockmen were. Another half hour and I heard, "Let's wrestle him down again."

"Oh no, you're out of lotion." That was my hope. The doctoring that I was getting was not like ice cream at a picnic.

Arling considered this with a chuckle, and came forth with a full bottle of the same stuff. "This one belongs to Woodrow and he's working on the Dixon ranch south of Buffalo Horn. Heck, he won't have to shave 'til spring." This time the lotion was rubbed in hard, and surprisingly the pain was not as sharp as it had been. Between treatments there were ideas kicked around about crutches for me, but then they thought the crutches should be for the horse. He was the one that fell down.

The big surprise came in the morning! The boot slipped on with just a bit stronger pull then usual. On the way to the barn I thought, "Praise be to the horse doctors and Aqua Velva."

For the next ten days Spike seamed willing to learn and I was willing to teach, so things went along on an even plane.

Due to Spike's education and my stiff foot we missed a show or two at the theatre in Hodgeville. The time came when we thought that a twenty-five mile round trip would add to Spikes learning.

After the movie, Basil, Hazel, Vivian, Berniece and I went to Wong's Coffee shop for coffee and a sandwich. We walked the girls home. Viv, Berniece and I were nearing the Mecalaw house, where the girls had their rooms, when Basil called, "I'll get the horses and meet you here."

"Don't let Spike get away and scatter my parka and chaps all over the country," I hollered after him.

"Oh no! He is too well educated to do that, and besides I'm too smart to let him do it." With a pal like that, who was a born winner, you just couldn't lose.

Viv said Good Night and scampered off. I stepped into the back porch to say Goodnight to Berniece. Basil was there with the horses real quick.

There were many houses, at that time, that had an outside entrance to the basement. It consisted of two doors at a slant from the wall off the house where they were about a foot high, and eight feet out, they were at the ground level. These covered the steps that led to the actual door in the wall of the basement. Mecalaw's house had this same kind of a door, only larger than most.

In the cold, Basil turned his back to the wind to tie his parka hood. He had Spike secured to his saddle horn. The horse showed good sense too, he turned his back to the wind and backed up a few steps, as far as his rope would allow. Klomp, Klomp, Klomp, Klomp. Now that was not good sense. Upstairs, Viv heard the horse's steps, looked out the window and held her breath. In the porch we heard the klomp klomp and that ended the goodnight ceremony right then. I eased the back door open real slow so I would not scare my horse into breaking through the basement entrance, but there was Basil gently leading Spike forward.

In short order I was in my riding duds and mounted. Berniece's voice always thrilled me, but when she called softly from the porch door, "Bernie did you know that your horse was standing on the cistern cover?" A pause. "Goodnight boys." Thrilled? Unh, unh. I was stunned! One inch of lumber between my horse and ten feet of water.

As the winter progressed, Spike proved time and again that he was of the self-destructing class. I thought we were well acquainted the day I rode off to get the mail. As I went past the house, our dog came out and nipped Spike in the heel. I was kind of relaxed, if my spurs wouldn't have caught the saddle skirts, I wouldn't have been riding. Oh boy, did that horse buck! The five-mile trip to town and five miles back with the mail took about the same time as Mother needed to slap the ham in the pan and set it on the table.

The next scrape that horse got into was the day I drove home from town and Spike was tied out in the sunshine. Joann and Woodrow explained.

Woodrow stopped by and when he was putting his horse in the barn, Spike turned and clowned around until he tipped himself over in the manger, and landed on his back with all four feet in the air. It took Woodrow and Joann a bit of time to get the rescue party organized. Joann sawed on the top two planks at one end of the manger while Woodrow swung the axe at the other end. That dumb horse was in big trouble. When enough wood was demolished, Woodrow cinched up his horse, threw a loop on Spikes front legs, dallied the lariat on the horn and pulled the poor horse out of the manger. It took about fifteen minutes before he could do more than roll his eyes. After a nudge he got up and they led him out to stand in the sunshine.

In May, as Spike was growing more hair to replace that which he left in the manger, Jack came for his horse.

"Thanks for breaking my horse," said Jack.

"Thanks for letting me use him for the winter," I replied. That ended our deal.

Spike just could not measure up to cow work. The following winter Jack rode him with the coyote hounds. Spike complained about carrying coyote carcasses behind the saddle. He would kick or buck or both.

It was ironic that a horse with that name would step on a board with a rusty spike in it. It penetrated the frog in the hoof, leading to infection. In just a few days, Spike was nibbling grass in the Happy Hunting Grounds.

Shorty L

Orvil did not want to become a farmer. Moving the wires to trip the corn planter, so the plants could be cultivated four ways, was of no interest to him. Nor did cultivating the corn seem to be to his liking.

"If you are determined to be a motor mechanic, I will pay for your schooling at the Auto School in Kansas City." This offer was made by Orvil's father.

Cousin Orvil acquired the nickname Shorty, and that is what he has been called for most of his ninety-three years. Shorty finished high school in the spring of nineteen eighteen. That autumn found him in Kansas City. The first year of school went just fine. Shorty loved the innards of an automobile. When the term was finished there was a grand, formal graduation exercise. Shorty as the honour student was handed the first diploma.

"That is no good to me," Shorty brashly refused.

The Dean was taken aback! No student had ever before refused a diploma. "What is wrong with it?" quizzed the learned man.

"Nothing wrong with the certificate. It's me." Shorty answered. "I know how to change a coil, but what goes on inside of one? I can align front wheels, but why does castor, and camber figure into the program?"

"If you are that dedicated, you need another year of school," the dean said and went on to the next student.

Next thing Orvil knew, he was back in Illinois cultivating corn for his room and board. In August the mention of a second bursary, from Pop, was met with screams of anguish.

"I gave you one whole year of school. Now you are on your own,"   .

Shorty was soon back in Kansas City. He was not destitute, but far from well to do. Days of searching brought good fortune. Near school he got a job in a bakery. The work hours were from 2:00 a.m. to seven o'clock in the morning. The bakery catered to early shift industrial workers, with coffee and fresh baked rolls. He could eat all he wanted at work and take a roll for noon and one for the evening meal. The wages just covered the educational cost.

More searching got him a bed in the attic of a nearby home in exchange for driving the old couple around in the evening in their new Ford car. This precarious lifestyle was a worry to Shorty. If one small part of it was lost, everything was lost!

One day in March, Shorty got to work, had a snack, and did the cleaning. He then mixed the dough and had two large pans of rolls rising, ready for the oven in an hour. About 4:30 a.m. he found that the rolls were covered solid with red ants.

"Hey boss what can I do?" The baker took one long look.

"There is nothing you can do. It is too late to start another batch. The men will need rolls. Pop them in the oven right now."

At 5:45 the rolls were brought out of the oven, a beautiful golden red glaze across each pan.

Next morning the customers, one after the other, asked, "I'd like a roll like you had yesterday, the ones that had the spicy covering."

The proprietor explained to each one, "Shorty made a mistake yesterday, and used all of the secret ingredient."

"Well when he can get some more secret stuff, I'll have them rolls."

The ants were a big hit, but Shorty did not know where they came from, or where to find any more. Though they did secure his job.

Early one Saturday morning, Shorty and the landlord and landlady were cruising down a highway. The plan was to visit her sister about an hour's drive out in the country. It was a great day, but half way home the landlord had studied Shorty's skills enough to do it himself. He got behind the wheel.

Nearing the city Shorty advised, "Better slow down some." The new driver just put on more speed.

"There is a main intersection just ahead. You will have to stop for it." This again came from the peanut coach in the back seat. This advice was not taken. It called for more speed. A Negro minister with a new Ford car, with its top folded down, like the landlords, entered the intersection. He was two steps ahead of the landlord. There was a mighty crash, the new driver with his new car, hit the other vehicle broad side. Both cars were a complete loss. Also lost were most of the chickens that were in the two crates that the minister had tied across his car just behind the front seat.

Most of those birds sharpened up their flying skills real fast. The clergyman got what local help he could for his chicken roundup. The other three went home by streetcar. Shorty, feeling that his job was over, packed his suitcase

"What are you doing?" asked the lady of the house. "You have kept your part of the bargain. We will keep ours. Get your things upstairs, because you have a room here as long as you like. If that old fool husband of mine wants to wreck his car, it is not your problem."

That is how Orvil got his diploma in May 1920.

Poor Horse

That fall I was three or four years old. Boy, oh boy, was I lucky.
I had helped Dad oil some binder chains. All I had to do was hold the oil
can with both hands, get a thumb on the pump lever and squirt oil. If I
was able to get any oil on one of the grain binder chains, it was just luck.
It was great helping Dad, until the oil can went dry. I requested a refill.

"No you are dirty and oily enough now. We will both be in
trouble with your mother," he said.

Later that morning, the four horse team was hitched to the
binder and harvest was under way. It must have been a successful start.
The field being harvested was close to the house, and with regular timing
I would hear the binder coming closer. Then the sound would fade away
to the north end of the field. I was forbidden to go through the shelter
belt of trees to watch.

After the noon meal and rest, harvest was resumed. I was
caught by the compulsory nap. When I woke up, I went outside. It was
hot and still, with hardly an insect on the move.

What was that? I heard it again. Yes a hammer banging on
iron, and in the field right close to the house. The latch on the yard side
gate was out of its notch. That was as good as an invitation to explore.
There was a small opening in the trees and there I saw the harvest outfit
just a short ways away.

I remembered the forbidding of the morning, but this was
afternoon and I had not gotten a new warning. The binder was standing
still. Dad and Bert, the hired man, were fixing a broken chain. I bravely
walked right up to help. Dad handed me three bundle twines. These
were trial run loops. I was also told to stay out of the way. I was well out
of the way, swinging my twine treasures, when Nettles, the goofy bay
mare, turned her head and saw me past her bridle blinds. She thought
that she should jump out of her harness. I was told to go home. The tone
left no room for argument. "And tell your Mother to latch that gate."

Passing the unlatched gate, I went to where the binder had been
that morning. The twelve foot long piece of twine was still there, just

laying on the ground. Grasping the long piece of twine, I returned through the unlatched gate. Mother got the message about the gate, while she used her pairing knife to cut my long twine in two.

Rover, our black and white Collie dog, was stretched out on the shady side of the house. He was not too excited about waking up, but sat on his haunches while I selected a loop that fit around his neck. So far, so good. Now all I had to do was tie a twine on each side of the neck band, and I would have driving lines. This was accomplished with some difficulty. My knots left much to be desired. Father had left his gloves in the porch. I went to borrow them for driving my shaggy black and white horse named Rover. The fact that I would need another fifteen years of growing to fit the gloves did not strike me as being important, but to be a real he-man I needed gloves.

Getting back to the dog, who was asleep again, but still harnessed up, I gathered up my lines and said GIDDY. Rover just laid there.

A nudge in the rear with my shoe brought more results. He got up and I drove him around to the front door, where he wanted to lie down again. We had an argument. He was supposed to turn left. After enough tugging on the lines, Rover merely turned to face me. He backed up a few steps and the harness came off over his head. He slunk away. I followed and tried to explain how a good horse was supposed to act.

We went around the house, through the peony beds, around the house again and through the flowers. Then I caught him in the fence corner. Before the harness was replaced, the obstinate beggar backed up and wrestled away. The game of tag was picked up again. The dog led and I was IT. I then found one glove was missing. In desperation I threw the other one at my would be horse.

I screamed, "You stupid dog. When I get big enough to drive real horses in the field I wont even let you come along."

Abe

We were moving south on No.19 highway at a reprimandable speed. I was in a hurry to get home. To Len, it did not matter that much. Then I hit the prairie chicken that busted out the right side high beam light on the Chev. It was not that serious. There was still the low beam light on that side. Assessing the damage showed the sealbeam and the chicken would never work again.

"I think it's about time for food," Len suggested.

"Yup. It's 7:30. I think you are right," I agreed.

Len Dillworth and I had spent most of the day looking at hay land in the Outlook Irrigation region.

"Let's stop at Elbow for supper," Len suggested. I thought that was the best idea I had heard all day. No doubt about it, the pork chops, vegetables, mashed potatoes and gravy, with a promise of apple pie and ice cream sure was good.

Partly through the meal, a tall rawboned character helped himself to a chair and sat down at our table.

"Hello Len. It's been a long time." He said.

"Hello Abe. I knew you were still alive, but I didn't know where. Meet my neighbour. He lives on the south side of the hay flats." Neither of us stood up. We shook hands across the table. Abe went on to explain that he too had spent some time in that area;

"Years ago I worked at Rush Lake. Yup, for the Z Bar Ranch, but that was before Smith took over. One morning, we came out of the bunkhouse and saw the foreman's horse tied to the corral, with his saddle on the top rail. I told Pete we should put the horse in the barn and feed him grain because the boss would most likely use him again that day.

We were riding in near sundown when the boss told me there were SPOOKS in the barn. Last night when he opened the door, one brushed against his face. 'I'll give you twenty bucks if you get him out of the barn for good. I got to go to Waldeck. I'll see you tomorrow.'

Pete and I tied our horses outside and sneaked into the barn real quite. There was no sound at all. We went outside to plan. Pete said, `Spooks won't make a sound.' I said, `You go back and listen real good. We need whiskey. I'll go and find some.'

When I got back with a bottle of the boss's whiskey, Pete came out and said he heard a whisper sound in the back corner by the old chop bin we don't use any more. We had a big drink. I got a baseball bat. Pete, he was short, so he took a pitch fork with lots of tines. We took another big drink. Then we made a plan to get in the old feed bin from the hay loft. We climbed up there and finished our whiskey. We moved the board off the hole in the floor. I said, `Here goes. Pete, you come too,' and I jumped in the hole. Pete came and we started swinging the ball bat and pitch fork. It was very dark and dusty but after awhile it was all quiet, so we kicked the door open. We killed so many bats that it took two five gallon pails to clean up the mess. There was two more clinging to the ceiling so I told Pete, `You get them. I'll go and find us another drink.'

In the morning the boss asked about the spook. I said he was gone for good. He gave Pete and me each ten dollars.

Then I told him it was so big and dirty and scary a job that we had to use two bottles of his whiskey before we got done."

During a visit with Ed Harrison, I causally mentioned Abe. Not only did Ed know Abe, but he told me the following;

"I know that man. He is a natural born horseman. They said even as a kid he had a collection of good horses. They were all spoiled animals that no one else could handle. He got them for next to nothing, but got them to do anything he wanted. Abe was just a kid, still living at home with his folks near where the river swings north. It was in the nineteen twenties that someone left a gate open, and the ranch cattle got out and destroyed about four hundred dollars worth of crop. The ranch had to pay the bill but Sandy, the foreman, blamed Abe. He was always riding through the pasture to go see friends near the river.

One day Sandy spotted Abe moseying along the trail. He rode fast to get to where he would intercept Abe near the gate. Even though

Sandy kept to the low ground, Abe was aware that he was being followed. Finally Sandy was out on the road and the faster he rode the faster Abe went. A quarter of a mile from the gate Sandy took down his lariat. When he shook out his loop, Abe saw what trouble he was in for. That's when the race became serious.

Sandy could not get close enough to rope Abe. Sandy's big bay gelding that was work hardened and grain fed was carrying more weight than Abe's little sorrel mare with the white socks. When they came to the gate, Abe did not slow down but leaned forward in his saddle and pulled up on the reins. The little mare sailed over the gate like a bird. Just beyond the length of a lariat rope Abe stopped and turned to his pursuer and hollered, `Sandy, don't forget to close the gate after you come through.'"

Ed and I had a good laugh over how a cocky young kid got the better of the ranch foreman. Ed went on to explain that Abe was the same in his senior years also;

He was 74 years old when three guys stopped at his place. They had an outlaw mare in the truck that they were going to sell for dog food. She was so wild and rank that it had taken them all morning to get her loaded. They had this horse tied every which way an animal could be tied. They warned Abe not to go near the truck because the horse was a killer, absolutely crazy. Now that was like waving a red flag at a bull. Abe was hooked.

In the house the host set a bottle of whiskey in front of these guys. "You fellas help yourselves. I got to get some fresh air."

Abe walked around the truck and talked to the mare, then reached in and petted her. Within a half hour he was leading her around the yard. Abe joined his guests for a small snort.

"That horse you got in the truck is in poor shape. How much do you think you'll get for her?"

It seemed that the owner did not expect to get very much.

"I'll give you that much for her," Abe offered.

"Oh no. You are an old man. She would kill you."

"Well let's go out and have a look at her," Abe suggested.

"O.K., but don't go near the truck. She's dangerous." When the three horse haulers got out in the sunlight they couldn't believe their eyes. Abe had the outlaw mare standing calmly tied to the garden fence.

There was a picture in the paper of 75 year old Abe leading the sports day parade riding the beautiful palomino mare that had been the outlaw only the summer before.

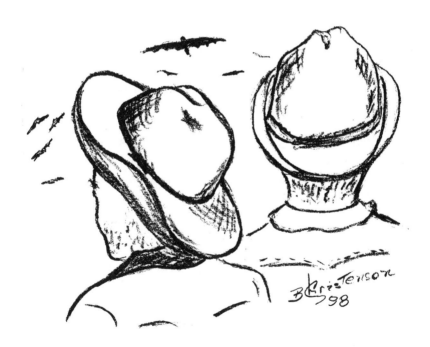

Storm

Oh, how it rained. For a few moments it fell in sheets, then it was all clear, but the dirt road was so muddy that by today's standards, it would be considered impassable.

A week before that June evening, on an island in the Polynesian chain, a tiny little bug that was so small one could hardly see it with a naked eye, wiggled a blade of grass. The events that followed could only be synchronized by nature. A bigger mite saw the grass move, with a downward spiral it pounced on the victim. A little predator fly whipped down and caught the mite. The hungry killer wasp dove in and swallowed the fly. Its end came when a wren dived to eat the wasp. The cute little wren was taken by the eagle that plummeted, from a great high perch. This sequence of events was positioned and timed perfectly. The nucleus of the air turbulence was brought on by the wee mite. Every creature involved gave size and power to the vortex.

This whirling little funnel was carried out to the Pacific. There, a huge albatross dove to the hart of the vortex with the hope of finding a fish dinner. When it departed with its tremendous wings flapping, it reinforced the spinning air to a point where it could grow by itself. Across the ocean the air mass gathered moisture. When it reached land, it was a great blue cloud. As it crossed the Rockies, it turned to a big blue black terrifying storm cloud.

In the 1940's a local dance had to have a ticket taker at the door. In our town, that was usually Ed. The polished floor would have a good sprinkling of dance wax. On the stage would be a three to six piece band. Often there was a lady at the piano and a guitar, violin, drum and a banjo. Oh yes, there was always a saxophone. It depended on each band as to the instruments they chose. Sound systems were unheard of. The melody and rhythm of the band filled the hall and set toes to tapping.

On each side, going the length of the hall were benches. The girls sat on the left side, and the boys on the right side. If a couple were on a serious friendly basis, they maybe sat together. The ladies, young

224

and not so young, were all groomed to the last degree. It was the former group that held most of our attention. Their hair was curled with not a wisp out of place. Their cosmetics were just right and their dresses freshly ironed. They all looked as much like the silver screen stars as they possibly could.

The men were not to be out done. Dress suits, white shirt and tie, and shoes with a brand new polish. Us just past adolescence, were there to impress the beautiful girls. Our faces were somewhere between handsome and ugly but were freshly shaven. Our hair was greased down and slick. Suits had a sharp crease, both trousers and jackets. A white shirt and tie were a must. Our aim was to look dashing.

That night my pal and I were on our way to the dance. We had steady girl friends and were anxious to see them. The strong wind that came up was not too bad, but when we reached the hills the rain started coming. The road became very slippery. It got so bad that we had to take turns pushing the car. We would push on the back to help it move forward, and then we would push on the front end to move it back on the road.

Every slithering step spattered more mud on us. When the wheels did spin, wet dirt came and went in every direction, and landed on us.

The tornado passed miles to the north and the rain storm had rumbled on east and left us with a cool wet evening. Reaching the big hills, we stopped to consider our chance of getting to town. We noticed a strange thing about colour. The mud on my brown suite looked gray but on Basil's blue suite it looked brown. Our neckties were muddy to say nothing of the rest of our clothes. We were two of the dirtiest boys that you would ever see.

Retreating toward home, unspoken, uncomfortable thoughts assailed each of us. When the orchestra had their hour off at midnight, would our girls go to lunch with some hot shot Romeo's? Then would they also escort them home? And kiss them goodnight?

All these jealous thoughts and mental torture just because a little bug wiggled a blade of grass in Polynesia.

225

Just Talk

Saturday morning. Ahead on the gravel road I spotted him, walking so portly and erect. He was wearing his Blue ball cap, smart suit jacket, baggy soiled denims and size ten white running shoes that were nearly run out. Yes that would be my Cree neighbour Simon, on his way to town. I stopped and offered a ride. Our Spruce Creek Ranch was snuggled in between the Forest reserve and the Pelican Indian reserve. We had to use the Indian road to get off the ranch.

We took care of the weather during the slow drive to the pavement. The road was badly rutted in places. The polite chit-chat, seemed to be finished, so we covered a mile or two in silence.

"Simon, did you ever work in the beet fields in Alberta?"

"Oh sure. I go tree times."

"Did you ever talk to the Blackfeet or Peigans?"

"Sure all time," he seemed so definite with his answer.

"Is the Blackfoot language the same as Cree?" I asked.

"No. No same. All deferent."

This rather puzzled me. Ben Fox was from the Blood Reserve. Archie Bigswan was ranching on the Peigan, and I had heard bits of their conversations. It sounded to me like there were two dialects.

Around a few curves, and up and down a few hills, and I was still pondering the Native Language Connection.

"Are there some words that are deferent in Blackfoot but you can understand them in Cree?" I asked again.

"No same. All not like." Simon answered.

"Well if they are so deferent, how did you talk to the Blackfeet?" I was searching for an answer for this one.

Simon, setting so erect with his arms folded across his chest, his nose pointed at a sophisticated angle, and with a devilish twinkle said, "We talked Englis."

Taxi

Bob Doake owned the livery barn. It was in the latter part of March in 1919, that the two cattle buyers from Winnipeg came to the livery barn. It was about 10:00 a.m. They needed a rig to drive to the ranch country.

"We'll need a fast team because we have to be on the 4:30 CPR Eastbound."

Bob was not impressed, "Do you guys realize that is more than seventy miles out there and back. I haven't got a team that I would drive that far in six hours. What you guys need is one of them new fangled Airoplains." This did not meet with cheers from the cattle buyers. Bob had a second thought. "Maybe Jake could make the trip with his car." Jake, a stable hand, was called into the confab.

"We want to get out to a couple of ranches northeast of here, to see some steers. But we also want to catch the 4:30 train. We'll give you five buck each."

Jake was agreeable to the offer. "I'll get my car and we'll give 'er a try." With that he went sauntering up the street in the direction of his bachelor shack. A short time later he had the decrepit old model T Ford Touring car, minus its top, parked by the water trough. While he was pouring water into the radiator, the buyers come up with a different offer.

"If you can get us back to get on the train at 4:30, we will go double or nothing."

"Back here by 4:30 and I get 20 bucks. If it is later than that the trip is on me. Sounds fair to me," Jake said. With the deal made to everyone's satisfaction, Jake finished filling the radiator and set the pail down beside the water trough.

Then a voice from a few steps away called, "Hey there you Wiellers men, what are you guys doing out here?"

The man at the front of the car exclaimed, "Well if it isn't Iky Cohn. We have just hired this man to take us out to a couple of ranches so we can look over some fat steers."

227

Mr. Cohn smelled a free ride, "Well I came out yesterday to see them animals too."

"Come on with us," said the Wiellers man that wore the jacket and Stetson. "We are paying five dollars each. We will be back at 4:30 on a double or nothing scheme. If you want to come on these terms, you're welcome."

Mr. Cohn thought this over for some seconds. "I want to be here by 8:00 p.m. I'm going on to The Hat tonight. But I'll go with you anyway."

The Ford puttered right along, and Jake, with some effort, kept his car between the fences. Closer to the ranch country they came to a coulee that ran north to the river. It had to be crossed. There was a snow bank that the winter wind had piled below the crest on the west edge. The water from this melting cliff of snow caused the two deep, muddy ruts that led to the bottom of the coulee. Jake aligned his wheels with the tracks and eased the car down the hill. It could be a problem on the return trip he thought. If he had to wait for frost, even 8:00 p.m. would come too soon. The east side of the coulee was dry but rutted. It posed no problem for Jake and his rattle trap of a car.

At the first group of cattle, the Wieller men took a quick look and said, "Here is our offer. Let us know in a few days if your boss agrees with this price." And handed the cattle man a notebook page with the figure penciled on it. Mr. Cohn just looked. It was too big a bunch for his company. At the second herd the Wieller men said, "Here is our offer let us know in a few days." Mr.Cohn seemed to want to get acquainted with every steer. He was really using up time to insure a free ride.

"Ike you have three minutes to finish your business here," called Bill the Wieller rep with the Stetson. His partner, John, wore city clothes with a navy blue overcoat. Jake had considered the road home. Going west, the slippery hill might be impossible to climb. The time was getting mighty short. The south road would be all right except for the grade across the slough. It too may be impossible. Mr. Cohn was at long last installed in the front passenger's seat. He checked his watch: it was past three o'clock. Jake turned south. Full speed ahead. He wound and rattled through the hills with his relic of a car. Travel in this part of the country with it's poor roads was usually avoided. At last, he came to the narrow grade that crossed the slough.

The only thing to do was pull the gas lever all the way down the spark lever down some, push down the low band peddle, and hope. About halfway across the muddy stretch of road the car could not move another inch. Mr.Cohn was enjoying the scenery. In the rear seat Bill and John were not overjoyed.

At the edge of the slough was a big brown horse nibbling at the dry grass. Jake stopped his motor, and got out of the car. Casually he walked up to the horse, took it by the mane and led it back to his Ford that was stuck in the mud. Backing the animal close to the front of the car, he tied its tail to the bumper. Cranking to get the motor running, he got in and said, "GEED UPP." The horse leaned into the load, towing Jake and company to dry ground. With a "WHOA," everything stopped. Jake untied the horse tail from car, led the animal to the side of the road, gave him a thank you pat on the neck and jumped in the car.

From there on, he called for all the speed the old tin lizzy had. At 4:20 they were parked in Herbert at the CPR station. Mr. C. wore his bowler hat down as far as his ears would allow. He was not smiling. The Wieller man Bill was waving his hat like he had just won a race all by himself.

His partner John said, "Well Iky that tow job was worth five bucks extra." Iky did not hear. "Fifteen dollars Ike. Or you may never buy another cow while we are around"

Iky heard. Handing over the said amount, Mr. Cohn mumbled, "Good Day gentlemen." The Wieller men paid their money and slapped Jake on the back and ran to board the eastbound.

There stood Jake the stable hand with forty five dollars in his hand. Nearly three months wages in one day. And the old brown horse nibbling the dry grass away out by the slough didn't even know that he had saved Jake's bacon.

Teeth

It was high up along the Fraser River, about the middle of British Columbia. Sixty yards from the saw mill site, was the edge of the ravine. At the bottom of this hollow grew a large fir tree. With the boss's blessing, Woodrow and I climbed from limb to limb toting along the equipment. A pulley, in it's cast iron frame, the piece of chain, a bolt, two wrenches and the end of the one hundred and fifty feet of cable.

The plan was to attach the pulley high in the tree, run the cable through the pulley and hook one end of the cable to the bundle of slabs and edgings at the mill. A team of horses on the other end would whisk the unwanted by-products into the ravine. This accomplishment was for the benefit of Earl.

We felt sorry for the white haired teamster. Due to one error, he lost his job on the railroad just a few years before retirement. For the last number of years he had drifted from one sawmill to another in Alberta and British Columbia.

We did not bother consulting Earl before we did this good deed. He had a bad stomach, and when it acted up it seamed to affect his disposition. The next day when the slabs had to be disposed of, Earls stomach was bad. He kicked at the cable that was in his way and snarled. Wallace the mill boss saw this, so he took the time to explain the contraption and it's use.

One night in the bunkhouse, Earl admitted that at first, he was not sure the thing would work, but it really did saved steps and time. "Thank you guys a lot," He said.

After months of mill work the ravine was level with slabs. Earl's stomach was giving him trouble again, and the cable was getting a lot of kinks and twists. One afternoon he was having trouble unhooking the cable from the slabs, so I went to help him. It was very quite, the mill was stopped while the sawyer filed the head saw. The crews were resting nearby. As I approached the spot that used to be the deep part of the ravine, but was now filled with slabs, Earl looked up from his problem. On this day his stomach was bad. Real bad. It looked like he was going to start swearing, but instead of cuss words, it was his upper denture that came out of his mouth. In the silence at the edge of the dark green forest I heard the top half of his eating machinery go rattling down and down to the very bottom of the slab pile.

With a stunned look, he removed the lower plate, and shoved it in his hip pocket, and drove his team back to the mill. Regaining a bit of composure he took one mitt and dusted the snow off of a fir stump. Bending himself into the shape of a bow string, (with his hips forming the angel where the arrow would be), he plopped himself down on the frozen stump. He yelled "WOOOOOO" and straightened up like a fresh shot bow string. His next move was to take the teeth out of his pocket and stomp on them.

Three nights later in his bunkhouse, he revealed the ugly red blotch on his hip. It was the shape of a very small horse shoe.

I could not help but blurt out, "Son of a gun! You were bit by your own teeth."

I had the presence of mind to get on the other side of the bunkhouse door real quick.

Speeding Ticket

Are you not astonished when a stranger says, "That is a darn poor spot on the earth where you live."

One Sunday night Berniece and I were trying out our 1952 Pontiac. That is how we come to be in Moose Jaw, Saskatchewan. It was still early. Darkness had just settled in, so we took a few minutes to visit Dot and Harry. Winding our way to the River Park district, Harry's highway tractor parked by the house meant that they were at home. Dot's father was also there.

After the introductions he asked, "Where do you folks live?"

"In Regina."

"Where at in Regina?"

"In the twenty two hundred block - Rose Street."

"What a ---- poor ---- ---- ---- where you live."

That set me back on my heels. This old fella that looked like a shrivelled, gray, twisted chunk of rawhide, bad mouthed our clean residential street.

He explained: I had taken up land west of Gull Lake, Saskatchewan. In 1913 I had to go to Regina to the Land Titles Office. It was in early April. The grass was starting to come up. The frogs were singing, but we had no mosquitoes. Instead of getting on the train in Gull Lake, I nailed summer shoes on my driving team and drove into Swift Current. The weather was so nice, so I drove on to Moose Jaw. My team still had a pretty sharp edge on their manners so I drove on to Regina. I had plenty of time and it was nice to get away from the homestead for a while. You know that two hundred miles with a good team, on dry roads was not much of a trip in those days. I stabled my team and got a hotel room. For the next two days I was getting things done up at Land Tittles.

That evening, I went over and curried and brushed my team. Those horses had two days of rest, so it was time for some exercise. I hitched up to my buggy and drove south to College Ave, then east to Rose

St. I had to hold my horses in. They would shake their heads and want to go.

The big shots from that part of town were giving their ladies buggy rides. Now these dumb dudes were driving with check reins that pulled their horses heads up and back. And the horses with that handicap moved like they were stepping on eggs. My horses had a lot of Thoroughbred blood and the going fools had their heads up without check reins.

When I turned north on Rose St., I pulled my Stetson down and decided to show these plug hatted dudes what a real team was like. I braced my feet on the front board on the buggy and let 'em go.

I'm here to tell you that team stepped out fast, very fast. I was weaving in and out, missing their buggy wheel hubs by an inch or two. I sure could feel the spring breeze. I just got to the twenty hundred block and a mounted police whistled me down and gave me a speeding ticket.

That Rose St. is one ---- poor place.

Safety Measures

It wasn't a cold night. It was a few degrees above normal for January, and this was January 17, 1931. Uncle Ted was in the barn saddling a horse when the ranch foreman showed up.

"Where are you going tonight?" he asked.

"Oh, I thought I would ride down to the store and get the mail," Ted answered.

That was a needless question. The store was more than seven miles away. Even so, it was far closer than any other human habitation. The ranches along the Red Deer River at that time, were not exactly one on top of the other.

"I sure hate to see you put a horse on the trail to the store tonight. The snow in the breaks is three feet deep in a lot of places," the foreman said.

"Gee whiz, I had my heart set on getting the mail tonight," Ted replied.

"Well, I know it will be tough going. When I came home from Calgary this evening, the snow was moving to beat the band. I had to really step on the gas to get the new truck down through the drifts. In the road down to the ranch the snow was getting deep." The foreman had a good argument, but seeing the crestfallen face of Ted, he had a good idea. He continued, "Why not take the ranch truck and drive on the river ice?"

"Do you mean that, Jack? Would you let me drive the brand new truck to the store?" asked Uncle Ted.

"Why not, it has been driven a hundred miles now. Another fifteen won't hurt it."

"Dog gone it Jack, I'll take you up on that. I do want to get the mail."

"Well then, you go out on the hay meadow and get your speed up. Be doing at least forty miles an hour when you hit the river. Drive with your hand on the door handle. If the truck goes down, jump as far away as you can. Don't worry about the truck, but save yourself. You better take it easy when you go past the ferry to get back on the road."

The saddle was returned to the tack rail, the men took the kerosene lantern and walked to the shed where the 1931 Model A, Ford Pickup Truck was parked.

"Ted look at the door handles. They don't turn like the old Chevy did. These pull instead of twist. Don't forget that if you crack the ice."

Jack stood with the lantern casting a feeble light on the winter snow. He watched and waited while Ted made the circle on the hay field then skimmed along the frozen river.

The ranch hand was in pure glory. The Ford fairly flew over the ice. One hand on the steering wheel, the other in the door handle. "At this rate, I'll have two extra hours to spend at the store! Whoopee!" Progress had been great. Over half the distance had been travelled when, Clunk! One rear corner went down. With a mighty leap, Ted left the truck to slide on his belly across the ice. There, a hundred yards away, the truck, minus it's left rear wheel, was doing crazy little circles on the ice.

The evening traveller that needed the mail so bad got the truck motor stopped, jacked up the vehicle and started to look for parts. Within a mile of backtracking he found the square key, the flat washer and lastly, the castellated nut, but no cotter key or hub cap.

With the gathered up parts laid on the running board, the hunt for the wheel began. The snow cover on the ice was spotty but it made it easy to track the runaway wheel. When the truck stopped going forward, the wheel kept right on going at forty miles an hour. It's path led straight down the river for part of a mile, to the edge of a small island where the track vanished.

Ted tramped over every square yard of the island and found no wheel. He went on the ice around the island, in ever widening circles. There was no mark of the wheel leaving this little bit of land. Crisscrossing through the poplar and willows from different angles didn't bring results. Going back to the spot where he last saw a wheel mark, he was convinced that the wheel had come this far right up to the log on the shore. In utter weariness he looked out on the island to the crows' nest in the willow clump.

"Hey, what the heck? Crows don't build nests in willows when there are poplar trees so close," he thought.

It was the Model A Ford wheel that was nested up in the willow. When it came to the log, it must have jumped and flew through the air to stop up in the willow branches. The wire spoke wheel, tangled in the willow twigs, was a problem to shake down.

While replacing the wheel, Ted said to himself, "If this had happened to Jack on one of the curves coming through the river breaks, he could have rolled to the bottom and he would have been killed. So would this new truck be dead.

With the repair done barehanded, by feel instead of light, Ted had cold hands. He started the truck. Standing in the glare of the headlights, he got out his pocket watch that kept time very well.

"Son-of-a-gun, two o'clock in the morning. I could wake up Mr. Weirver at the store and get the mail, but his sister Pauline, who is visiting from BC, will be in bed by now. I don't think there was any mail anyway."

PS   Two years later, Pauline became Mrs. Ted Muri - Aunt Pauline to me.

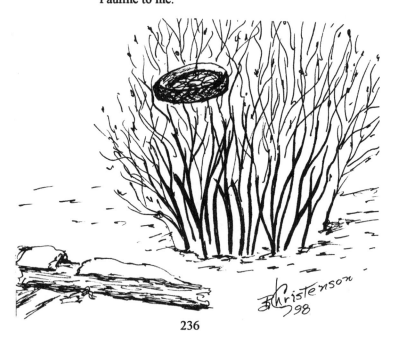

236

Good, Bad and Others

Axle's life style was changing. Not that he strove for change, it more or less just took place. The husky young man had no aim in life. He was a product of the time, moving from one farm to another plowing, blacksmithing, shoeing horses or just plain labouring. At retirement time in the middle of the century he was changing. It had been years since he had pilfered any item or cheated at poker. Hard liquor very seldom passed under his mustache. Instead of a stiff drink, he often settled for a cup of tea with Widow Pirkens. He was definitely changing.

Satan was well aware of the change. He wanted Axle's soul. Mrs. Pirkens wanted Axle. To tip the scales in his favour, Satan assigned his henchman Ploy, to the task.

Ploy asked for an appointment with St. Peter. "I have no time for that scummy devil. St. Thad, you see what he wants."

St. Thad did not relish the task. It never was a joy to deal with any spirit from the underworld.

"Well, whatcha want?" With a greeting like that, Ploy was not surprised. At the gate of heaven, their group never did get the "How Do You Do Sir" welcome.

"I want to go to the village of Daisy Creek and live with Axle for a month, he needs me." Ploy begged.

"In a pigs eye, he needs you." Thad snorted.

"Well, how about it can I go?"

"For a month! Are you nuts?"

"Oh at least a month."

"How about a day?" Thad had weakened a bit.

After a reasonable amount of bickering and quibbling, six days was the allotted time. St. Thad was a sharp negotiator. The terms were rigid.

One: Only five minutes each day you can be in Axle's house.

Two: This permit is good only from eight A.M. until midnight.

Three: You can operate only in the town limits but not across the tracks where the grain elevators and oil tanks are. And the town park, too, is out of bounds to you.

It was the best deal he could get, so Ploy signed on the dotted line.

"Just remember Ploy, one step over the line and Poof, you're gone."

The first day was half gone before Ploy materialized on the street of Daisy Creek. He had planned on being on the job earlier but he spent an hour in the vacant shed at the edge of town. It took a lot of rectal muscle contraction to get his tail pulled into where it could fit into his disguise. The horns were a problem too, but when they were turned and pressed against his scalp, he could get the greasy old Stetson pulled down to his ears.

Axle sauntered along Grain Ave. with no particular thought in mind, and with no particular destination either.

"Hello there Axle, it's been a long time." There was Ploy with his hand begging to be shook.

Axle shook hands. With a quizzical look he said, "I just don't seem to place you, right off."

"Joe Shanks, remember we worked together on Smiths steam outfit, thrashing in 1928."

"Ya I was on Smith's crew in 28 but I just can't remember you."

Ploy had made his first move, now, for the second. Eyeing the tavern door he said, "For old times sake let me buy you a drink."

Axle thought, well, nothing wrong with a couple beers this time of day. He hadn't completely accepted the Pirkens life style. Seated in the barroom, Axle did not introduce his new found friend. Ploy had to handle that little chore himself. To one and all he announced I'm Joe Shanks an old buddy of Axle's. From table to table Ploy did the gentlemanly handshake, "Howdy, Ben, George, Pete, Hank, Bud, Elmer."

Elmer became the thorn in the flower bed! With bleary blue eyes and a trembling chin he inquired, "You can't be Joe Shanks, you aint old enough to be him and you be too old to be one of his kids."

"Oh ya! I'm Joe Shanks."

238

"The Joe Shanks I knew was hanged for murder, when I was a whipper snapper back east. That was about '18 or '19. I come west in 27."

"No, it wasn't me"

"But, you sure resemble the Joe Shanks they hung." It seems to happen to Devils, Angels and People that have to use thin disguises. There is always someone who will try to put a hole in the balloon. In this case, it was Elmer that was the know-it-all. The longer Elmer thought about it, the more of Joe Shank's past came to mind. He remembered the arrest of Joe Shanks, and with his squeaky voice enlightened all the patrons. Joe Shanks disclaimed it all. The longer Elmer combed his brain, the more proud he became. The trial, conviction, and gallows were remembered and retold. Yes, Joe Shanks had been a skunk, but he paid in the end.

Ploy ignored all this oration. To himself, 'The old fool sure would like to blow my cover. It was a mistake to take my former human shape.' Ploy bought round after round of drinks. To the pensioners, this was a financial boost to have a generous gent in town. All but Axle, he had his reservations. Dusk was settling over Daisy Creek. Heavy wet March snow was falling. Axle was, due to Ploy's poisoned drinks, profoundly and completely drunk

"It's time to go Axle," Ploy was the ever so kind protector. As they teetered from the table, Satan's man pushed a glass on the floor. Axle stepped on it. "Clink," it broke and cut a large S shaped gash in Axle's rubber boot. Ploy put his arm around Axle's waist and helped him to the door. On the sidewalk Axle's cut left traces of blood on the fresh snow. That track with it's smear of red could be followed all the way to Axle's shack. Ploy laid Axle on his bed, put a lump of coal in the stove, stole Axel's rubbers, flipped the night latch, slammed the door and was gone.

Morning of the second day, Widow Pirkens was absolutely mortified. Where her walk met the village sidewalk, someone with a badly cut rubber, left a trace of blood in the foot print, and had urinated a disgusting yellow ring in the snow. Mid morning the word was spreading. "Axle cut his foot." "Did you hear Axle cut his foot." "Axle

239

stepped on a beer glass and cut his foot." "Axle's foot is cut so badly that it bleeds when he walks."

Axle was the only person in town that did not know about the cut foot. His foot was all right, it was his head and stomach that gave him the pain. Mrs. Pirkens was in a very foul mood as she shovelled her walk. That was not like Axle to do a thing like this, but still there it was, and his cut foot. For the rest of the day her mood swung between indignation and sympathy.

In the late afternoon Ploy called at Axle's house. "Knock, knock,"

"Go away. I don't feel good." At least Axle's voice was strong and clear. Satan's imp made his way down the street to the Ford garage. As though he knew the in's and out's, he walked right into the back corner of the parts room. Introducing himself as an old friend of Axle's, he invited himself into the Black Jack game. Two hours later he had lost four bucks, and established a reputation as a real gentleman, with the card players.

The third morning the Pirkens lady was enraged! Some low brow had made the yellow ring in the snow half way up her walk, and with that cut up rubber sole track right there too. Oh how disgusting! Axle went to the store for a hand full of groceries. Ploy called to him but all he got was a high snoot ignore. Axle still had a pain in the head and he suspected Mr. Joe Shanks was to blame. Ploy had planned on the two of them being at the Black Jack table.

Morning four, had bright sunshine. It was frosty, but with a promise of spring. It should not have been busy, but it was. This morning found troubles coming to a focal point. Axle could not remember ever working with Joe Shanks. Mrs. Pirkens was at a loss as how to stop the yellow spots on her walk. St. Thad had his hands full watching Ploy. Axle was out to get some fresh air. He was on the street beside the park when he saw the man running and heard the shots.

The Smith Bros. each had a load of grain at the U.G.G. elevator, just waiting for Max to open the doors. They were standing by their trucks when they saw the man running and heard the shots. The CN track crew was getting ready for work, They saw and heard it all. Max was the closest to the park. He had just passed the corner and started across the rail road track when the sound of gunfire completely cleared his head of sleep.

Moments before the shots were fired, Mrs. Pirkens glimpsed him through the kitchen window. She was horrified. There beside her house was a man with his shoulders slightly hunched, his head down as though he was looking at his shoes, and making a yellow spot beside her walk. Ploy had to hurry before someone spotted him. It was just eight o'clock and his day had begun. When he heard the back door slam, Mr. Joe Shanks took to his heels. When Ploy heard the back door slam, he had to get the heck out of there. It would upset his whole plan if Mrs. Pirkens found out that it was not Axle that was peeing on her walk. He raced down the walk, across the street and made a terrific leap over the hedge to land him in the park.

Pirkens, with her long departed husbands Winchester 12 G.U. loaded with goose shot fired both barrels at the runner, BANG BANG just as Ploy was leaping over the park hedge.

St. Thad was watching. "Ploy you have stepped across the line." Poof, he was gone.

The Pirkens person was so wrathful, she muttered as she turned to her house, "I don't care if I blew him to hell." Little did the good woman know that with St. Thad's help that is exactly where he went. With Axle, the Smiths, Max and the CN crew the shot gun blast was heard and the shooting was witnessed from four angles. "Mrs. Pirkens shot a man." "Did you hear dear Emily shot at some intruder?" "I heard that she missed." "How could such a small woman use a double barrel shot gun that good?" And so the news grew and spread like wildfire.

When they found that it was Joe Shanks that got it, the old guys at the bar and the Black Jack players went into five minutes of mourning. Some guys didn't give a hoot. .

The RCMP, from the neighbouring detachment came to investigate. All they could find in the fresh white snow were a pair of rubbers, (one badly cut by stepping on a broken beer glass) and a dirty, old, tan coloured Stetson. No body, no tracks, absolutely nothing, not even a trace of a murder.

Sunday evening Reverend and Mrs. Fimore and Axle were guests of Mrs. Emily Pirkens.

What Were They?

The one room country school was a place where we farm kids went to get educated. Row one was the farthest from the cloak room doors. The seventh row of desks was closest to the wall that had the boys and girls cloak room doors. The biggest kids sat at these desks. I suppose that was a safety measure, so us little guys in row one, two and three would not get trampled in the recess stampede when everyone rushed to the great outdoors.

In three years, I had moved from row one to row three. There were five grades of students and four rows of seats between me and the openings to the bright fresh air. Our teacher was a large girl, big boned, with an angular frame.

Generally her disposition was sweet and feminine, but when conditions warranted she could match an ox driver that used a long black bull whip. On this day, she was getting pretty eloquent telling us about the pioneers with their covered wagons with a plow tied on the side and the milk cow tied behind. Over the unknown, untracked sea of waiving grass etc., etc. I was bored, it was the same old stuff that she had taught Olive and Beatrice two years ago, and I had heard it then.

"Bernard! Pay attention." She continued, "Leaving loved ones behind, and going purposely into a strange new land," then with an edge on her voice she said, "Bernard, do you not want to learn about the pioneers? Your grandfather was a pioneer."

"Nope. He was a homesteader," I corrected her.

With the patience and tone of someone explaining a deep theory to an imbecile she said, "Your grandfather was one of the first people to take a farm in this area. Therefore, he was a pioneer."

"Nope." I replied.

"Stop that slang. The word would be no," she corrected me.

"In the States he was a pioneer," I added.

"He was a pioneer here," her voice had a soprano sound.

"He was only twenty five miles from the railroad, and telegraph, and the livery barn and the hotel, so he was just a homesteader."

242

With a red face and a sound like a fire truck she said "PIONEER." With that, she put the text book down the same way a farmer with a spade would slap a rat into the ground. She took a deep breath and went on to the next class. I figured that she did not win the argument, just terminated our discussion.

Ole was a young, Norwegian blacksmith. He was tall. He was a person that stood above everyone else in a crowd. But crowds were pretty scarce in those days. The area consisted of Grandpa on the south ridge, Billy south of the creek and Ole on the other side. Oh sure there were others but the landscape was not near overrun.

Billy was the very opposite of Ole. Grandpa said that Ole was strong enough to knock down a work horse. He had a Copenhagen pocket in his lower lip, because he always chewed snuff. Billy was short beside Ole, he had a scar on his upper lip that made a little twist beside his nose. He had an accent too. It was very easy to understand. Mom said that he got it at collage.

Billy could open my grade three math book to any page and just say the answers without hardly thinking. But Ole could knock down a horse.

It was fifteen years before my time that the thunder clouds roared on the horizon where Wiwa creek had its beginning. The storm seemed to have swung south by bed time. The next morning, the ground was damp, even a bit muddy so Billy pulled on his rubber boots and crossed the creek on the stepping stones. By the middle of the morning he had finished his errand and was on his way home. The stones that he had stepped on in the morning were now under about five feet of swirling flood water. There were no bridges on Wiwa creek at that time. Billy had no choice but to go to Ole for help or advice. Ole's hut was only a hundred yards from the crossing. His feet drug and his spirit slumped. Less than a month ago he had told the dumb Norwegian about herd laws and animals at large, and a lot of other things. Explaining to Ole the predicament of five feet of water to a four and a half foot tall, non swimming man was rather humiliating.

"Yu shoor, I cood cary you across," was Ole's ready answer and they returned to the creek. With Billy sitting on Ole's shoulders, he waded into the water. When they were chest deep and Billy could feel the cool water against his boots, Ole stopped. He thought this might be a good time to ask, "You remember the time when my horses got in your oat field?"

Billy's reply was rapid and excited, "Yes, yes. I've been meaning to talk to you about that. It really is no big deal."

"Yu dats what I thought," said Ole and waded to the south shore.

The Telephone Co., the Co-Op, the Wheat Pool all in later years had Billy as secretary, and Ole as chairman or director. Be darned if I know now. Were they Pioneers or Homesteaders?

Absolute Zero

I picked up the mail and went across the street to ROBIN'S NEST. My snow suit had a pitch or sap smell plus other assorted odours, so I sat at the counter rather than at a table or in the lounge. Helen served coffee with an explanation, "See the clock? It says that in two hours, I'll start three full days off. That is why I can show all my teeth in this big smile." Then Rob came along with a "Hi-There," and leaned his arms on the counter.

"Say Rob, do you know the inner workings of a kerosene or propane fridge?"

"Well I have some knowledge of their principles," he admitted and then continued, "The heat from the flame expands the Freon gas, which in turn forces the gas through a venture, that causes a pressure imbalance, which chills the condenser, resulting in extraction of heat from the fridge. The end result is refrigeration."

"Well could you use the sun to power an air conditioner?" My question was just a lead up to the big one that I was going to ask next.

"Oh of course you could but it may not be feasible."

"Well if we can turn heat into cold why can't we reverse the process and get some warmth out of all this cold air," I asked.

"No. That would be impossible. Really there is no such thing as cold, it is the absence of heat that you feel today. Heat as we know it is truly kinetic energy, or you could say molecules in motion. The greater the molecular action, the higher the temperature. At minus two hundred and seventy three point nine nine nine degrees C, and that is cold, there is practically no movement of the atom, but there is still some. If you could cool an object to absolute zero, it would cease to exist. The proton and neutron would not form an atom, so in theory the entire structure of the thing that was at absolute zero just would not be." Rob continued, "Take the power line as an example. It starts out at Squaw Rapids at maybe four thousand volts. I don't know what it is when it reaches the transformer out here, but there it is cut to two hundred and twenty volts. If there was a way to super cool the power line, they could maybe start it at the source at say three hundred volts and when it reached us we would not need a transformer, you would have the two twenty. The colder the conductor the less resistance there is."

I said with a dumb simile, "It sure is easier to cross a corral full of cows when they are laying quite rather than when they are all heated up and moving all around. Maybe it's the same with electricity when the atoms are still."

"There is a lab in France where they have, with the use of liquid nitrogen, super cold electromagnets which have tremendous power. An atom can be sent down this tube at near the speed of light. Just about, but not as fast as the speed of light. This is in the same class problem as absolute zero. If anyone could reach either one of these goals, that person would be very famous." Rob was definite with that statement.

"Back to your first question. No! There is no way known to mankind to change cold to heat."

"Well thanks Rob, see yu next time I'm in town." On the road back to the ranch I could tell that it was cold, the air was so sharp and clear that I could nearly see individual trees out on the Birch Lake Ridge. They were large trees but miles away. The cows too could tell it was cold. They certainly did justice to the fifty heavy alfalfa bales I fed them. In the house I unlaced my bushpac boots, unzipped my snow suite and hung it up, and licked my chops. Supper was on the stove and it did smell good.

"Dear where is the flour and sugar?" asked my wife.

"Ohmygosh. I forgot to get the groceries." I used the universal excuse

"You forgot? Boy if you aren't an ABSOLUTE ZERO."

Say now this could pose a problem. Would Berniece be famous for the discovery? Or would I be famous for being it? Or would I cease to exist?

Slippery Sam

Years ago, Furseths had been our neighbours across the fence. This was after each of us had lived in a couple of different communities. Les and I got together for a coffee one day. It was mentioned that the bank was leaving our town after eighty two years of service.

"Have you thought of doing like the guy that we heard about the morning we went to get your auction sale tractor?" Les asked.

One slow sip of coffee and I answered, "I could use the money, but living in town, the cows would be a problem."

This is what happened. Only the names have been changed to protect me.

Les had to be on his way home in the morning. On the way he had to pick up a load of alfalfa, or his cows would be out of feed on Thursday. Instead of going to bed Tuesday night we set out to get my tractor home. By the time we had driven the Mac and trailer a hundred and five miles, got Frank (the tractor's former owner) out of bed, jump started the Case and got it loaded on the trailer, it was no longer night. The northeastern sky had that 'here comes the dawn look'.

"You fellas come in for a coffee. I started the coffee perk before I came out. It will be ready now." Frank invited us in. We were nursing hot mugs around the kitchen table.

I turned to Frank and asked, "Who was that guy with the gray striped overhauls at your sale that was bidding on everything but did not buy much?"

"That was Sam. He used to live near here." Frank looked out the window at the dawning sky then the wall clock which indicated three o'clock. "That guy is as crooked as the day is long, and we've got long days. When Sam was a lot younger he and a friend got a bunch of stock certificates printed up, gilt edged and fancy but not worth a darn. These two got a spiffy new car, like an important person should drive. Of course this was with the smallest down payment possible. They also got dark pin striped suits and snap brim hats." As an after thought, Frank

247

said, "They used to go to the city to see gangster movies. That was where they learned to dress so smart. Sam and his pard hit the road and sold these shares. They worked hard and sold countless sheets of paper for ten dollars each. When they had the country saturated, they moved north. The last I heard, they were selling to the Indians for a dollar a share. When they ran out of their fancy paper, they hi balled it to the States.

In time, the court was after an extradition order so that Sam and his pard could be brought back to Canada to face fraud charges. Sam heard of this and showed up at the police station in a bad frame of mind. He grumbled about not letting him know that they wanted him, "And why didn't you call me? I could have straightened the whole thing out over the phone." Well the officers told him to stay around and they would see him in a few days.

His next move was to the bank. There he said he needed money to hire a good lawyer. The d---- police had this trumped up charge against him. If he only had eight thousand dollars, he would sure show them! The manager arranged to go out to check his collateral the next morning. When the banker got to the farm, Sam pointed out this old black and white cow in the yard. He said that's my cow and there is seventy five more over there in that field and a hundred more over in the other field and still more over north. They made out the loan forms at eight thousand dollars and two hundred head of cattle as security. That afternoon Sam went to the bank and got eight thousand dollars cash, and scooted right back to Nevada.

When the time ran out for the court on the phony shares charges against him, Sam came home. The bank could not touch the cattle that were seen in the fields on that other spring day. They belonged to the people that owned that land. The bank did get Sam's old scrawny gut sprung Holstein cow."

Frank finished the story by saying, "I don't think he has been able to borrow a dollar since."

Looking across the table at Les the other day, I said, "I don't think they make bankers like that any more."

248

Farmers

The soil was moist, light and sandy. The weeds didn't stand a chance. Round after round, the brown earth had turned over to leave the unwanted vegetation buried. I had to have more fuel before I could finish the work on the south farm.

Putting a barrel on the deck of the Ford three ton, I started for town. I would have to hurry to get there before closing time. About ten miles down the road, I came to a truck parked off to the side. Two men with two flat tires stood beside it. The introductions were fast and informal. I threw the flat tires on my truck, asked the two gentlemen to climb in, and we raced the remaining eight miles to town.

I dropped the men and tires off at the garage and as I headed toward the fuel tanks, I hollered to them, "I'll be back in a minute, I need my barrel filled!"

At the garage the men were told, "You go and have supper. We'll have your new tires ready when you get back."

I got my fuel, and then headed over for supper. Over pork chops at Seto's coffee, I got better acquainted with my passengers. Charlie farmed and ranched a ways to the southwest. George had farmed near him, but forty years ago he sold the farm for peanuts he claimed, and moved to BC. Now he had two years before the railroad would pension him off.

I thanked Charlie for the meal and we returned to the truck. The sun had swung to the west. The beautiful summer day would end with a colorful sunset.

There didn't seem to be any rattlesnakes in the weeds beside the truck. The truck owner and his friend were possibly thirty-five years older than myself, so I grabbed a wheel to put on the far side. The truck wasn't high enough, and Charlie's jack wouldn't lift it any further. It took some maneuvering to get my jack into position to raise the vehicle, but I got that tire on and the bolts snugged up. The left side rear tire looked like it was in rough shape so Charlie decided that the new spare should be put on to replace it.

We jacked the left side up, and faced defeat. Charlie's wrench wouldn't loosen the wheel bolts, and mine wouldn't fit. Help came when Nick stopped his new half ton by us. No problem, he could get it off.

As Nick took his tools out to start changing the tire, George was telling us how hard he had to work when he used to bury rocks to make a buck or two in the homestead days.

"One time a guy asked me to get rid of a stone that was about five feet high. I sized it up and marked out the hole I would have to dig. I had the hole dug down about seven feet, and figured that would be enough. I would go and dig around it up on top. While I crawled out the south side of the hole, the rock rolled in from the north side. That was it, all I had to do was shovel the dirt back to cover the rock."

Charlie just shook his head, "George you were crazy to take a chance like that."

George didn't respond because he was admiring Nick's new red tool box with the three quarter inch drive socket set.

"I sure envy you guys today with hydraulic jacks and shiny wrenches." George went on, "It was a crime, what we had to put up with in the early days. When you paid three hundred bucks for a new plow, you got one flat wrench that fit five or six bolts. It was flat and short so you could not get a bolt really tight. You had to check the plow over for lose bolts every time you stopped to rest the horses."

By now Nick had the wheel on and tightened. He looked at George and said, "You were complaining? Before my Father came to this country, he farmed with one small steer hooked to a crooked stick."

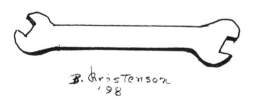

B. Kristenson
'98

The Black Mare

"Yes sir, she was the fastest thing on four legs. At least she could outrun anything in our part of the country."

Ed had his booted feet, with heels and spur counters, resting on the livingroom carpet, his toes pointed to the ceiling. His long legs, stretched out from slim hips in the big arm chair, gave him a look of ease. The blue plaid shirt and western style jacket covered broad shoulders. He had gray hair, smooth tight skin over high cheek bones, clear bright eyes, and with a thin white mustache, he made the perfect picture of a retired cattleman.

He continued, "The race track around Lundeen Lake was a half mile long. When that little black mare was running, the only question was who would come in second and third."

"It was years later that I found out the facts about that black mare. By that time the mare was grazing in the forever pasture and the kid had grown to be a heavy middle aged man. His mother told me their story.

"We were farming and raising a few cattle in Kansas. My husband was a good horseman.

Them boys, like Billy the Kid, Butch Cassidy, the Younger Brothers, Frank and Jessie James and that kind of citizen, were experts. They were right at the top of the heap when it came to handling guns. Pistols first and rifles second. As for horses, they were not only the best riders, but they were also the best judges of horseflesh. These guys needed fast, tough, solid bottom horses.

If they were slow with guns and rode slow horses, they never got to be very bad men. You can see the reason for that.

We had a black mare that my husband was awfully proud of. She was fast, strong and could run all day.

One day my hubby Joe was in town with his mare. He had tied her in a corral behind the livery barn. There was no cost just to tie up in the back. He had just left the barn when Jessie James and some of his gang rode in. This bunch was about a quarter of the people in town and four times as tough, so they felt sorta safe. They announced that they didn't want trouble, just an afternoon at the saloon. Suddenly, the sheriff found official business out of town.

Jessie was riding a black stallion that he put up in the livery barn.

When the James people got into the bar room, my Joe said to hisself, "If that horse is good enough for Jessie James, it's good enough for me." He untied the stallion and took him out back and serviced his mare, then tied him back with the same knot that Jessie had used.

The next summer our mare had the little black filly that grew into the mare you asked about.

The next fall my husband and his black mare were both killed in the same accident. Well, range in Kansas was scarce and we were being crowded. We were small and the big outfits on one side and scratch dirt farmers pushing in on the other side, gave us the same hope as a snowball . . . you know where. With Joe gone it was terrible."

Ed said, "The old lady let her mind role back over the years and went on."

"We knew about the land in Canada, and the police system. We loaded two carloads of cows and heifers, and one carload of horses and the boy and I came to Canada. That little black mare was in that car."

When Ed finished the story, he nearly had a tear in his eye.

"That Joe was mighty brave to get a colt that way. She was brave too, for a woman to load up her animals and bring them and her son to Saskatchewan took a lot of guts. They sure deserved every measly dollar that the kid and mare ever earned on local race tracks."

252

The Road Block

There were small ripples on the lake. The few white fluffy clouds were mirrored in the water.

"The Aspen leaves are waving, but not turning over, so there isn't any rain today," Jack observed. The rest of the group was on the lawn in front of the cabin. Their conversations had centered on their field of work which was hospitals, health, medicine and all of the modern rights legislated to save mankind.

Jack and I sat on a log near the shore and he told me the following civil rights case.

One time a guy ran out of a bank in Regina. There was a fella waiting at the intersection for the light to change. The runner jumped into the car with this guy. It seemed the driver had to share his car with a bank robber, the man had a bag in one hand and a gun in the other.

The robber shouted, "Drive me to the States or I'll blow your brains out!"

Minutes later, the Plymouth two door hard top stopped at a service station at the outskirts of the city. Upon being served gas, the same command was given. "Drive away or I'll blow your brains out!"

That was a mistake, the attendant saw the gun at the drivers head. Now gas station owners don't like drive aways that haven't paid. Because this guy had a gun to his head just made the call to the police even more urgent. It was an open and shut case. The fugitive had robbed the bank and was fleeing to the States with a hostage. Near Weyburn the road block was in place.

The maniac with the gun shouted, "Let us by, or I'll blow his brains out!" They let him go.

At the border crossing the swat team was in place. The same old threat, so they let him go. Well into the states, there was a big contingent of police. The Plymouth came to a stop. The blue automatic pistol was pressed to the driver's temple. The same threat with the same results, they let him go.

The crook tried a secondary highway. Now they were rid of all the swat teams and road blocks. Back in the hills the local sheriff, listening to his radio got wind of the hostage taking. His road block was simple. He turned his patrol car across the road and stood beside it. When the men in the Plymouth stopped, he calmly walked up to the passenger's door. The robber had his gun to the driver's head. "Let us go or I'll blow his brains out!"

The old lawman pulled out his old bone handled Colt 45, put its mussel against the fugitive's head and said, "Go ahead, but you'll never hear the bang."

The bank robber dropped his gun, raised his hands and sat there trembling.

Jack concluded the story, "The old boy didn't know about all the rights people have now. He was of the old school, an `eye for an eye' type of cop."

The Coyote Laffed

Berniece and I drove among the Giant Saguaro cactus on the Arizona desert. Arriving at the National Desert Cactus Park, we were offered a seat while the tour group was gathered. A tall gray haired lady with her park rangers uniform, led us down the path. Our guide knew her business. She was a very interesting person. The humming bird house was first, a large screened room with trees and the birds.

We learned about every grass, bush and tree that we met. The guide was good. The path was forty five minutes long. Very interesting but, it seemed, that every time that I had a scene in my view finder, these two people were in my way. Or if I wished to hear the guide, there they were one on each side of me, loudly comparing this to the Atlantic region. They did not need the guide. They knew it all! By the time we got to the man made, many storied animal condominium, I was peeved. The obnoxious couple did not look good. He was short and fat and loud, she was tall scrawny and louder. I did get a picture of the puma, and the peccary.

Then Mrs. Ugly told me, "See down there, there is the coyoteee."

Before that I had glimpsed the half grown coyote pup, and I did not envy it, I replied, "Oh I won't bother looking, I've shot dozens of them." Mrs. Ugly turned back to me with the most horrid look on her face. I stepped back, I thought she would retch. That coyote pup was very sad.

*   *   *

I was hurrying to get the last of the hay baled. It was near midnight when the coyote walked out of the forest beside the meadow. He was a big guy, tall with creamy fur, nearly as big as a wolf. I stopped the tractor and stared at the animal. The tractor lights reflected the blue of his eyes. Such a blue I had never seen before. They were a jewel-like quality to say the least. With a laugh he went to look for the fat grouse.

*   *   *

I was just a kid with my first .22 rifle. After school, I climbed on a horse and went out to shoot a duck. The third pond that I crept up on, had no ducks, but there was a coyote. My nerves were so tense that I shook. At that distance, I could easily hit a tomato can. I aimed for a broad side shot, pulled the trigger and missed. The coyote laughed and trotted off.

*   *   *

Mother had a red and yellow rooster. Not an important bird, but he did crow at day break. That earned him the name of Squawk. One morning all was quite. Squawk was gone.

I had not started school, so I had lots of time for exploring. The stock pond was a half a mile from the house. Among the big willows I found the red and yellow feathers. That was all that was left of Squawk.

I waved my five year old fist and shouted, "You dirty old thieving skunk of a coyote"

The coyote hiding in the rose bushes, licked his chops and laffed.